■ SCHOLASTIC

Math Problem-Solving Packets

Mini-Lessons for the Interactive Whiteboard With Reproducible Packets That Target and Teach Must-Know Math Skills

Carole Greenes, Carol Findell & Mary Cavanagh

NEW YORK • TORONTO • LONDON • AUCKLAND • SYDNEY
MEXICO CITY • NEW DELHI • HONG KONG • BUENOS AIRES

Teaching *Resources*

Editor: Mela Ottaiano
Cover design by Jorge J. Namerow
Interior design by Melinda Belter
Illustrations by Teresa Anderko

ISBN: 978-0-545-45957-0

Table of Contents

Introduction

Welcome to *Math Problem-Solving Packets: Grade 6*. This book is designed to help you introduce students to problem-solving strategies and give them practice in essential number concepts and skills, while motivating them to write and talk about big ideas in mathematics. It also sets the stage for more advanced math learning—algebra, in particular—in the upper grades.

Building Key Math Skills

The National Council of Teachers of Mathematics (NCTM) identifies problem solving as a key process skill and considers the teaching of strategies and methods of reasoning to solve problems a major part of the mathematics curriculum for children of all ages. The Common Core State Standards (CCSS) concurs. "Make sense of problems and persevere in solving them" is the first standard for Mathematical Practice in CCSS.

The problem-solving model first described by renowned mathematician George Polya in 1957 provides the framework for the problem-solving focus of this book. All the problems contained here require students to interpret data displays—such as text, charts, diagrams, graphs, pictures, and tables—and answer questions about them. As they work on the problems, students learn and practice the following problem-solving strategies:

- making lists or cases of possible solutions and testing those solutions
- identifying, describing, and generalizing patterns
- working backward
- reasoning logically
- reasoning proportionally

As students solve the problems in this book, they'll also practice computing, applying concepts of place value and number theory, reasoning about the magnitudes of numbers, and more. In addition, they will learn the "language of mathematics," which includes terminology (e.g., *odd number, variable*) as well as symbols (e.g., >, <). Students will see the language in the problems and illustrations and use the language as they discuss and write about how they solve the problems.

How to Use This Book

This book contains six problem-solving packets—each composed of nine problems featuring the same type of data display (e.g., diagrams, scales, and arrays of numbers)—that focus on one or more problem-solving strategies and algebraic concepts. Each set opens with an overview of the type of problems/tasks in the set, the problem-solving focus, the number concepts or skills needed to solve the problems, the CCSS standard(s) covered, the math language emphasized in the problems, and guiding questions to be used with the first two problems of the packet to help students grasp the key concepts and strategies.

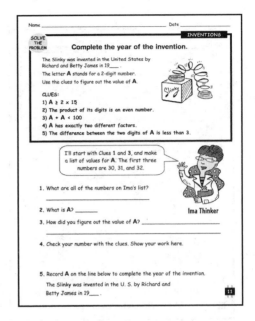

The first two problems in each packet are designed to be discussed and solved in a whole-class setting. The first, "Solve the Problem," introduces students to the type of display and problem they will encounter in the packet. You may want to have students work on this first problem individually or in pairs before you engage in any formal instruction. Encourage students to wrestle with the problem and come up with some strategies they might use to solve it. Then gather students together and use the guiding questions provided to help them discover key mathematical relationships and understand the special vocabulary used in the problem. This whole-class discussion will enhance student understanding of the problem-solving strategies and math concepts featured in the packet.

The second problem, "Make the Case," uses a multiple-choice format. Three different characters offer possible solutions to the problem. Students have to determine which character—Mighty Mouth, Boodles, CeCe Circuits—has the correct answer. Before they can identify the correct solution, students have to solve the problem themselves and analyze each of the responses. Invite them to speculate about why the other two characters got the wrong answers. (Note: Although we offer a rationale for each wrong answer, other explanations are possible.) As they justify their choices in the "Make the Case" problems, students gain practice and confidence in using math language.

While working on these first two problems, encourage students to talk about their observations and hypotheses. This talk provides a window into what students do and do not understand. Working on "Solve the Problem" and "Make the Case" should take approximately one math period.

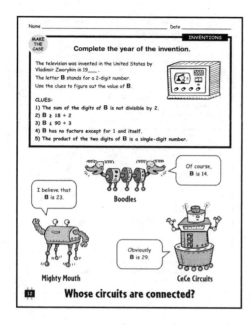

The remaining problems in each packet are sequenced by difficulty. They all feature a series of questions that involve analyzing the data display. In the first three or four problems of each set, problem-solving "guru" Ima Thinker provides hints about how to begin solving the problems. The rest of the problems offer no hints. If students have difficulty solving these latter problems, you might want to write "Ima" hints for each of them or ask students to develop hints before beginning to solve the problems. An answer key is provided at the back of the book.

The problem-solving packets are independent of one another and may be used in any order and incorporated into the regular mathematics curriculum at whatever point makes sense. We recommend that you work with each packet in its entirety before moving on to the next one. Once you and your students work through the first two problems, you can assign problems 1 through 7 for students to do on their own or in pairs. You may wish to have them complete the problems during class or for homework.

Using the CD

In addition to the reproducible problem-solving packets in this book, you'll find a CD with ActivInspire (Promethean) files* and PDFs of "Solve the Problem," "Make the Case," and "Solve It" problems, for use on the interactive whiteboard. (Black-line masters of these pages also appear in the book.) Display "Solve the Problem" and "Make the Case" on the whiteboard to help you in leading a whole-class discussion of the problems. Then use the additional "Solve It" problems to guide students in applying our three-step problem-solving process:

1. **Look:** What is the problem? What information do you have? What information do you need?
2. **Plan and Do:** How will you solve the problem? What strategies will you use? What will you do first? What's the next step? What comes after that?
3. **Answer and Check:** What is the answer? How can you be sure that your answer is correct?

These "Solve It" problems encourage writing about mathematics and may be used at any time. They are particularly effective as culminating activities for the problem-solving packets.

---

*If you do not have ActivInspire software on your computer, click on the folder titled **Promethean Installers**. To install the software on a Mac, double-click on **ActivInspire_v1.6.43277_USA.dmg** file, then click on **ActivInspire.mpkg**. If you have a PC, double-click on **ActivInspireSuite_v1.6.43277_en_US_setup_PC.exe**. Please read the PDF file for the license agreement.

The problem-solving packets in this book support the following Common Core State Standards.

MATHEMATICAL PRACTICES
1. Make sense of problems and persevere in solving them.
2. Reason abstractly and quantitatively.
3. Construct viable arguments and critique the reasoning of others.
4. Model with mathematics.
5. Use appropriate tools strategically.
6. Attend to precision.
7. Look for and make use of structure.
8. Look for and express regularity in repeated reasoning.

RATIOS AND PROPORTIONAL RELATIONSHIPS
Understand ratio concepts and use ratio reasoning to solve problems.
6.RP.2 Understand the concept of a unit rate a/b associated with a ratio $a:b$ with $b \neq 0$, and use rate language in the context of a ratio relationship.
6.RP.3 Use ratio and rate reasoning to solve real-world and mathematical problems, e.g., by reasoning about tables of equivalent ratios, tape diagrams, double number line diagrams, or equations.
    d. Use ratio reasoning to convert measurement units; manipulate and transform units appropriately when multiplying or dividing quantities.

THE NUMBER SYSTEM
Compute fluently with multi-digit numbers and find common factors and multiples.
6.NS.2 Fluently divide multi-digit numbers using the standard algorithm.

Apply and extend previous understandings of numbers to the system of rational numbers.
6.NS.7 Understand ordering and absolute value of rational numbers.

EXPRESSIONS AND EQUATIONS
Apply and extend previous understandings of arithmetic to algebraic expressions.
6.EE.2 Write, read, and evaluate expressions in which letters stand for numbers.
6.EE.3 Apply the properties of operations to generate equivalent expressions.
6.EE.4 Identify when two expressions are equivalent (i.e., when the two expressions name the same number regardless of which value is substituted into them).

Reason about and solve one-variable equations and inequalities.
6.EE.5 Understand solving an equation or inequality as a process of answering a question: which values from a specified set, if any, make the equation or inequality true? Use substitution to determine whether a given number in a specified set makes an equation or inequality true.
6.EE.6 Use variables to represent numbers and write expressions when solving a real-world or mathematical problem; understand that a variable can represent an unknown number, or, depending on the purpose at hand, any number in a specified set.
6.EE.7 Solve real-world and mathematical problems by writing and solving equations of the form $x + p = q$ and $px = q$ for cases in which p, q, and x are all nonnegative rational numbers.
6.EE.8 Write an inequality of the form $x > c$ or $x < c$ to represent a constraint or condition in a real-world or mathematical problem. Recognize that inequalities of the form $x > c$ or $x < c$ have infinitely many solutions; represent solutions of such inequalities on number line diagrams.

Represent and analyze quantitative relationships between dependent and independent variables.
6.EE.9 Use variables to represent two quantities in a real-world problem that change in relationship to one another; write an equation to express one quantity, thought of as the dependent variable, in terms of the other quantity, thought of as the independent variable. Analyze the relationship between the dependent and independent variables using graphs and tables, and relate these to the equation.

GEOMETRY
Solve real-world and mathematical problems involving area, surface area, and volume.
6.G.1 Find the area of right triangles, other triangles, special quadrilaterals, and polygons by composing into rectangles or decomposing into triangles and other shapes; apply these techniques in the context of solving real-world and mathematical problems.

References

Common Core State Standards Initiative. (2010). *Common core state standards for mathematics.* Washington, DC: National Governors Association Center for Best Practices and the Council of Chief State School Officers.

Greenes, Carole, & Carol Findell. (Eds.). (2005). *Developing students' algebraic reasoning abilities.* (Vol. 3 in the NCSM Monograph Series.) Boston, MA: Houghton Mifflin.

Greenes, Carole, & Carol Findell. (2005). *Groundworks: Algebraic thinking.* Chicago: Wright Group/McGraw Hill.

Greenes, Carole, & Carol Findell. (2007, 2008). *Problem solving think tanks.* Brisbane, Australia: Origo Education.

Moses, Barbara. (Ed.). (1999). *Algebraic thinking, grades K–12: Readings from NCTM's school-based journals and other publications.* Reston, VA: National Council of Teachers of Mathematics.

National Council of Teachers of Mathematics. (2000). *Principles and standards for school mathematics.* Reston, VA: National Council of Teachers of Mathematics.

National Council of Teachers of Mathematics. (2008). *Algebra and algebraic thinking in school mathematics,* 2008 Yearbook. (C. Greenes, Ed.) Reston, VA: National Council of Teachers of Mathematics.

Polya, George. (1957). *How to solve it.* Princeton, NJ: Princeton University Press.

Inventions

Overview

Students use clues and reason logically to figure out the value of the unknown represented by a letter. The value of the letter is used to complete the year of an invention.

Problem-Solving Strategies

- Make a list of possible solutions
- Test possible solutions with clues
- Use logical reasoning

Related Math Skills

- Compute with whole numbers
- Identify factors and multiples of numbers
- Identify odd and even numbers

Algebra Focus

- Solve for values of unknowns
- Replace letters with their values

CCSS Correlations

6.NS.2 • 6.NS.7 • 6.EE.2
6.EE.3 • 6.EE.4 • 6.EE.5
6.EE.6 • 6.EE.7 • 6.EE.8

Math Language

- Digit
- Difference
- Factor
- Multiple
- Remainder
- Symbols: Less than <, Less than or equal to ≤, Greater than >, Greater than or equal to ≥, Not equal to ≠
- Value

Introducing the Packet

Make photocopies of "Solve the Problem: Inventions" (page 11) and distribute to students. Have students work in pairs, encouraging them to discuss strategies they might use to solve the problem. You may want to walk around and listen in on some of their discussions. After a few minutes, display the problem on the interactive whiteboard (see the CD) and use the following questions to guide a whole-class discussion on how to solve the problem:

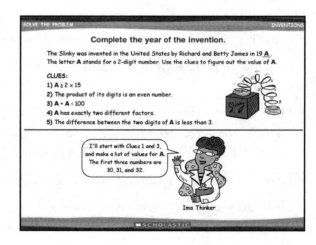

- Look at Clue 1. What does the symbol ≥ mean? *(A is greater than or equal to 2 x 15, or 30.)*

- Why did Ima use Clues 1 and 3 to make her list of possible values for A? *(Clue 1 gives the least number possible, which is 30. Clue 3 gives the greatest number possible, which is 49; 49 + 49, or 98, is less than 100.)*

- What are the numbers on Ima's list? *(30, 31, 32, . . ., and 49)*

- Which numbers on Ima's list match Clue 4? *(31, 37, 41, 43, and 47)* What are the factors of these numbers? *(These numbers have only 1 and themselves as factors.)*

- Which of the numbers that have two factors match Clue 2? *(41 because 4 x 1 = 4, 43 because 4 x 3 = 12, and 47 because 4 x 7 = 28.)*

- Which of the numbers 41, 43, and 47 match Clue 5? *(43 because 4 – 3 = 1 and 1 < 3.)*

- How can you check your answer? *(Replace each A in the clues with its value. Be sure that the statements are true.)*

Work together as a class to answer the questions in "Solve the Problem: Inventions."

Math Chat With "Make the Case"

Display "Make the Case: Inventions" on the interactive whiteboard. Before students can decide which character's "circuits are connected," they need to figure out the answer to the problem. Encourage students to work in pairs to solve the problem, then bring the class together for another whole-class discussion. Ask:

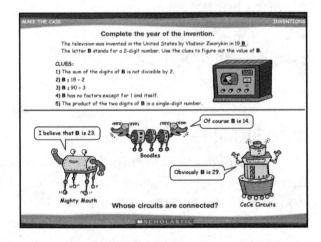

- Who has the right answer? *(Mighty Mouth)*

- In what year was the television invented? *(1923)*

- How did you figure out the value of B? *(From Clues 2 and 3, B can be 9 through 30. Clue 4 eliminates all numbers that have more than two factors leaving numbers 11, 13, 17, 19, 23, and 29. Clue 1 eliminates 11, 13, 17, and 19, leaving 23 and 29. Clue 5 eliminates 29.)*

- How do you think CeCe Circuits got 29? *(She probably ignored Clue 5.)*

- How do you think Boodles got 14? *(Boodles probably ignored Clue 4.)*

Name _____ Date _____

SOLVE THE PROBLEM

Complete the year of the invention.

The Slinky was invented in the United States by Richard and Betty James in 19____ .

The letter **A** stands for a 2-digit number.

Use the clues to figure out the value of **A**.

CLUES:

1) **A** ≥ 2 x 15

2) **The product of its digits is an even number.**

3) **A + A < 100**

4) **A has exactly two different factors.**

5) **The difference between the two digits of A is less than 3.**

I'll start with Clues **1** and **3**, and make a list of values for **A**. The first three numbers are 30, 31, and 32.

1. What are all of the numbers on Ima's list?

   _____

2. What is **A**? _____

3. How did you figure out the value of **A**? _____

   _____

Ima Thinker

4. Check your number with the clues. Show your work here.

5. Record **A** on the line below to complete the year of the invention.

   The Slinky was invented in the U. S. by Richard and

   Betty James in 19____ .

Math Problem-Solving Packets: Grade 6 © 2012 by Greenes, Findell & Cavanagh, Scholastic Teaching Resources

MAKE THE CASE

Complete the year of the invention.

The television was invented in the United States by Vladimir Zworykin in 19____ .

The letter **B** stands for a 2-digit number.

Use the clues to figure out the value of **B**.

CLUES:

1) The sum of the digits of **B** is not divisible by 2.

2) $B \geq 18 \div 2$

3) $B \leq 90 \div 3$

4) **B** has no factors except for 1 and itself.

5) The product of the two digits of **B** is a single-digit number.

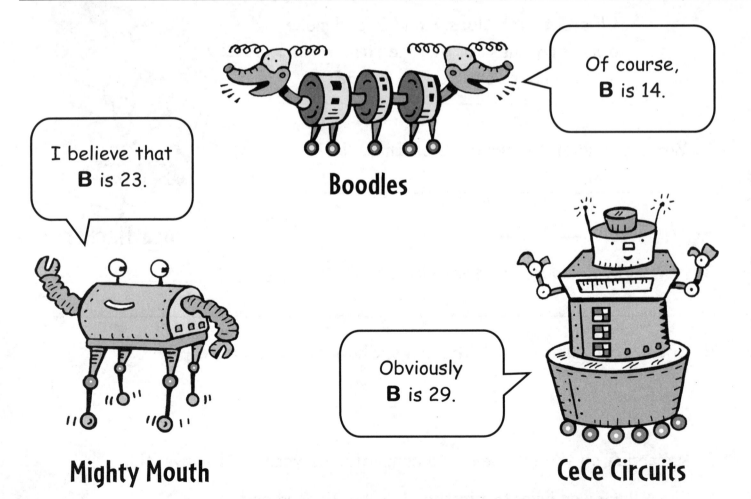

Of course, **B** is 14.

Boodles

I believe that **B** is 23.

Obviously **B** is 29.

Mighty Mouth

CeCe Circuits

Whose circuits are connected?

Math Problem-Solving Packets: Grade 6 © 2012 by Greenes, Findell & Cavanagh, Scholastic Teaching Resources

Name _____ Date _____

PROBLEM
1

Complete the year of the invention.

Post-it notes were invented in the United States by the 3M Company in 19____ .

The letter **C** stands for a 2-digit number.

Use the clues to figure out the value of **C**.

CLUES:

1) **C** is a multiple of 8.

2) **C** < 4 × 22

3) **The product of the two digits of C is zero.**

4) **C ≠ 40**

> I'll start with Clues **1** and **2**, and make a list of values for **C**. The first three numbers are 16, 24, and 32.

1. What are all of the numbers on Ima's list?

_____

2. What is **C**? _____

3. How did you figure out the value of **C**? _____

_____

Ima Thinker

4. Check your number with the clues. Show your work here.

5. Record **C** on the line below to complete the year of the invention.

Post-it notes were invented in the U. S. by the 3M Company in 19____ .

Name _____ Date _____

PROBLEM 2

Complete the year of the invention.

The Rubik's Cube was invented in Hungary by Erno Rubik in 19____ .

The letter **D** stands for a 2-digit number.

Use the clues to figure out the value of **D**.

CLUES:

1) **D** is an even number

2) **D** $\leq 150 \div 2$

3) **D** $> 7 \times 9$

4) **The difference between the digits of D is greater than 2.**

5) **The product of the digits is greater than 20.**

I'll start with Clues **2** and **3**, and make a list of values for **D**. The first three numbers are 64, 65, and 66.

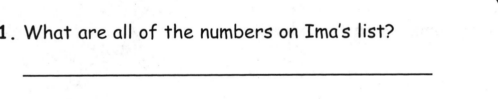

Ima Thinker

1. What are all of the numbers on Ima's list?

   _____

2. What is **D**? _____

3. How did you figure out the value of **D**? _____

   _____

4. Check your number with the clues. Show your work here.

5. Record **D** on the line below to complete the year of the invention.

   The Rubik's Cube was invented in Hungary by Erno Rubik in 19____ .

Math Problem-Solving Packets: Grade 6 © 2012 by Greenes, Findell & Cavanagh, Scholastic Teaching Resources

PROBLEM 3

Complete the year of the invention.

Pong was invented in the United States by Noland Bushnell in 19____ .

The letter **E** stands for a 2-digit number.

Use the clues to figure out the value of **E**.

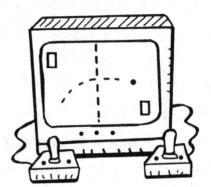

CLUES:

1) 6 is a factor of **E**.

2) **E** ≤ 10 × 8

3) **E** > 9 × 6

4) 8 is a factor of **E**.

I'll start with Clues **2** and **3**, and make a list of values for **E**. The first three numbers are 55, 56, and 57.

1. What are all of the numbers on Ima's list?

_____

2. What is **E**? _____

3. How did you figure out the value for **E**? _____

_____ _____

Ima Thinker

4. Check your number with the clues. S'.ow your work here.

5. Record **E** on the line below to complete the year of the invention.

Pong was invented in the U. S. by Noland Bushnell in 19_____ .

Name _____ Date _____

PROBLEM 4

Complete the year of the invention.

The cell phone was invented in Sweden by technicians at the Ericsson Company in 19____ .

The letter **F** stands for a 2-digit number.

Use the clues to figure out the value of **F**.

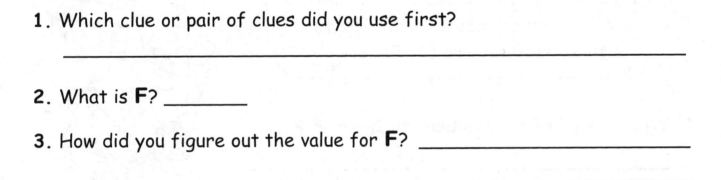

CLUES:

1) $F \le 9 \times 9$

2) $F \div 10$ has a remainder of 9.

3) The sum of the digits of **F** is an even number.

4) $2 \times F > 100$

5) $F \ne 59$

1. Which clue or pair of clues did you use first?

_____

2. What is **F**? _____

3. How did you figure out the value for **F**? _____

_____

4. Check your number with the clues. Show your work here.

5. Record **F** on the line to complete the year of the invention.

The cell phone was invented in Sweden by technicians at the Ericsson Company in 19____ .

16

Math Problem-Solving Packets: Grade 6 © 2012 by Greenes, Findell & Cavanagh, Scholastic Teaching Resources

PROBLEM 5

Complete the year of the invention.

The ballpoint pen was invented in the United States by John Loud in 18____ .

The letter **G** stands for a 2-digit number.

Use the clues to figure out the value of **G**.

CLUES:

1) **G** is a multiple of 11.

2) 2 is a factor of **G**.

3) **G** ÷ 3 has a remainder of 1.

4) 10 × 10 > **G**

5) **G** ÷ 5 has a remainder of 3.

---

1. Which clue or pair of clues did you use first?

_____

2. What is **G**? _____

3. How did you figure out the value for **G**? _____

_____

4. Check your number with the clues. Show your work here.

5. Record **G** on the line to complete the year of the invention.

The ballpoint pen was invented in the U. S. by John Loud in 18____ .

Name _____ Date _____

PROBLEM 6

Complete the year of the invention.

An accountant who worked for a chewing gum company
in the United States invented bubblegum in 19____ .

The letter **H** stands for a 2-digit number.

Use the clues to figure out the value of **H**.

CLUES:

1) **H** is a multiple of 4.

2) 60 > **H** + **H**

3) When you divide **H** by 3,
   the remainder is not zero.

4) **H** + ½ **H** ≥ 30

5) **H** ≠ 100 ÷ 5

---

1. Which clue or pair of clues did you use first?

   _____

2. What is **H**? _____

3. How did you figure out the value for **H**? _____

   _____

4. Check your number with the clues. Show your work here.

5. Record **H** on the line to complete the year of the invention.

   An accountant who worked for a chewing gum company in the U. S.
   invented bubblegum in 19_____ .

Math Problem-Solving Packets: Grade 6 © 2012 by Greenes, Findell & Cavanagh, Scholastic Teaching Resources

Name _____ Date _____

PROBLEM 7

Complete the year of the invention.

The pop-top can was invented in the United States by Ernie Fraze in 19____ .

The letter **J** stands for a 2-digit number.

Use the clues to figure out the value of **J**.

CLUES:

1) $J < 1 \times 2 \times 3 \times 4 \times 4$

2) Two of **J**'s factors are 3 and 7.

3) $J \div 2$ has a remainder that is not zero.

4) $J \neq (2 \times 2 \times 2 \times 3) - (3 \times 1)$

5) $(3 \times 6) + 2 \leq J$

1. Which clue or pair of clues did you use first?

_____

2. What is **J**? _____

3. How did you figure out the value of **J**? _____

_____

4. Check your number with the clues. Show your work here.

5. Record **J** on the line to complete the year of the invention.

The pop-top can was invented in the U. S. by Ernie Fraze in 19____ .

Perplexing Patterns

Overview

Presented with an array of counting numbers, students identify relationships among numbers in the rows and columns of an array.

Problem-Solving Strategies

- Describe parts of patterns
- Generalize pattern relationships

Related Math Skill

Compute with counting numbers

Algebra Focus

- Explore variables that represent varying quantities
- Use letters to stand for varying quantities
- Identify and describe the functional relationship between numbers in rows and columns of an array

CCSS Correlations

6.RP.3 • 6.EE.9

Math Language

- Array
- Multiple

Introducing the Packet

Make photocopies of "Solve the Problem: Perplexing Patterns" (page 22) and distribute to students. Have students work in pairs, encouraging them to discuss strategies they might use to solve the problem. You may want to walk around and listen in on some of their discussions. After a few minutes, display the problem on the interactive whiteboard (see the CD) and use the following questions to guide a whole-class discussion on how to solve the problem:

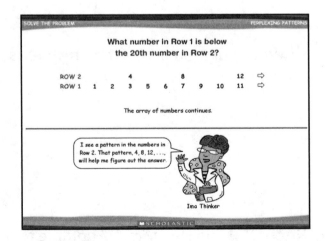

- What are the first three numbers in Row 2? *(4, 8, and 12)*

- What pattern did Ima see in these numbers? *(They are consecutive multiples of 4.)*

- What is the 4th number in Row 2? *(16)* The 10th number in row 2? *(40)*

- How did you figure out the 10th number in Row 2?
  (1 x 4 = 4, 2 x 4 = 8, 3 x 4 = 12, and so on; the 10th number is 10 x 4, or 40.)

- What number in Row 1 is below the first number in Row 2? *(4 – 1, or 3)*
  Below the second number in Row 2? *(8 – 1, or 7)*

- If you know the position of a number in Row 2, how do you figure out the number
  below it in Row 1? *(Multiply the position number by 4 and subtract one from the product.)*

Work together as a class to answer the questions in "Solve the Problem:
Perplexing Patterns."

Math Chat With "Make the Case"

Display "Make the Case: Perplexing
Patterns" on the interactive whiteboard.
Before students can decide which
character's "circuits are connected," they
need to figure out the answer to the
problem. Encourage students to work in
pairs to solve the problem, then bring the
class together for another whole-class
discussion. Ask:

- Which character has the right answer?
  (Boodles)

- How did you figure it out?
  (The 12th number in Row 3 is 12 x 5, or 60. The number in Row 1 below 60 is 60 – 2, or 58.)

- How do you think CeCe Circuits got the answer 60? *(She gave the 12th number in Row 3.
  She probably forgot to subtract 2 to get the number in Row 1 that is below 60.)*

- How do you think Mighty Mouth got the answer 59? *(He may have subtracted 1 instead
  of 2 to get the number two rows below 60.)*

Name _____ Date _____

SOLVE THE PROBLEM

What number in Row 1 is below the 20th number in Row 2?

ROW 2			4		8			12	⇨
ROW 1	1	2	3	5	6	7	9	10	11	⇨

The array of numbers continues.

I see a pattern in the numbers in Row 2. That pattern, 4, 8, 12, . . ., will help me figure out the answer.

Ima Thinker

1. What pattern did Ima see in Row 2? _____

_____

2. What is the 20th number in Row 2? _____

3. What number in Row 1 is below the 20th number in Row 2? _____

4. What number in Row 1 is below the 30th number in Row 2? _____

5. What number in Row 1 is below the 50th number in Row 2? _____

Math Problem-Solving Packets: Grade 6 © 2012 by Greenes, Findell & Cavanagh, Scholastic Teaching Resources

MAKE THE CASE

What number in Row 1 is below the 12th number in Row 3?

ROW 3		5		10		15		⇨
ROW 2	2	4	7	9	12	14	17	⇨
ROW 1	1	3	6	8	11	13	16	⇨

The array of numbers continues.

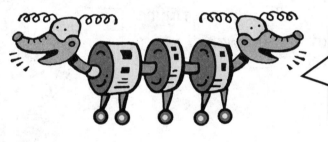

Surely you can see the number is 58!

Boodles

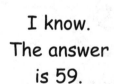

I know. The answer is 59.

Mighty Mouth

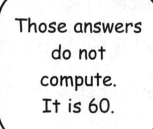

Those answers do not compute. It is 60.

CeCe Circuits

Whose circuits are connected?

PROBLEM 1

What number in Row 1 is below the 15th number in Row 2?

ROW 2		3		6		9		12	⇨
ROW 1	1	2	4	5	7	8	10	11	⇨

The array of numbers continues.

I see a pattern in the numbers in Row 2. That pattern, 3, 6, 9, . . ., will help me figure out the answer.

Ima Thinker

1. What pattern did Ima see in Row 2?

_____

2. What is the 15th number in Row 2? _____

3. What number in Row 1 is below the 15th number in Row 2? _____

4. What number in Row 1 is below the 25th number in Row 2? _____

5. What number in Row 1 is below the 30th number in Row 2? _____

Math Problem-Solving Packets: Grade 6 © 2012 by Greenes, Findell & Cavanagh, Scholastic Teaching Resources

Name _____ Date _____

PROBLEM 2

What number in Row 1 is below the 10th number in Row 3?

ROW 3			6		12		18	⇨
ROW 2		3	5	9	11		15	17	⇨
ROW 1	1	2	4	7	8	10	13	14	16	⇨

The array of numbers continues.

I see a pattern in the numbers in Row 3. That pattern, 6, 12, 18, . . ., will help me figure out the answer.

Ima Thinker

1. What pattern did Ima see in Row 3?

_____

2. What is the 10th number in Row 3? _____

3. What number in Row 1 is below the 10th number in Row 3? _____

4. What number in Row 1 is below the 15th number in Row 3? _____

5. What number in Row 1 is below the 20th number in Row 3? _____

PROBLEM 3

What number in Row 1 is below the 30th number in Row 3?

ROW 3			7			14			21		⇨
ROW 2	2	4	6	9	11	13	16	18	20	23	⇨
ROW 1	1	3	5	8	10	12	15	17	19	22	⇨

The array of numbers continues.

I see a pattern in the numbers in Row 3. That pattern, 7, 14, 21, . . ., will help me figure out the answer.

Ima Thinker

1. What is the 30th number in Row 3? _____

2. What number in Row 1 is below the 30th number in Row 3? _____

3. How did you figure out the answer to #2?

   _____

4. What number in Row 1 is below the 40th number in Row 3? _____

5. If you know the position of a number in Row 3, how can you figure out the number below it in Row 1?

   _____

Math Problem-Solving Packets: Grade 6 © 2012 by Greenes, Findell & Cavanagh, Scholastic Teaching Resources

PROBLEM 4

What number in Row 1 is below the 20th number in Row 4?

ROW 4			9			18			27		⇨
ROW 3		5	8		14	17		23	26		⇨
ROW 2	2	4	7	11	13	16	20	22	25	29	⇨
ROW 1	1	3	6	10	12	15	19	21	24	28	⇨

The array of numbers continues.

1. What is the 20th number in Row 4? _____

2. What number in Row 1 is below the 20th number in Row 4? _____

3. How did you figure out the answer to #2?

_____

4. What number in Row 1 is below the 25th number in Row 4? _____

5. If you know the position of a number in Row 4, how can you figure out the number below it in Row 1?

_____

Name _____ Date _____

PROBLEM
5

What number in Row 1 is
below the 24th number in Row 4?

ROW 4				10				20			⇨
ROW 3			6	9			16	19			⇨
ROW 2		3	5	8		13	15	18		23	⇨
ROW 1	1	2	4	7	11	12	14	17	21	22	⇨

The array of numbers continues.

1. What is the 24th number in Row 4? _____

2. What number in Row 1 is below the 24th number in Row 4? _____

3. How did you figure out the answer to #2?

_____

4. What number in Row 1 is below the 30th number in Row 4? _____

5. If you know the position of a number in Row 4, how can you figure out
   the number below it in Row 1?

_____

Math Problem-Solving Packets: Grade 6 © 2012 by Greenes, Findell & Cavanagh, Scholastic Teaching Resources

PROBLEM 6

What number in Row 1 is below the 30th number in Row 5?

ROW 5			8			16			24		⇨
ROW 4			7			15			23		⇨
ROW 3			6			14			22		⇨
ROW 2		3	5		11	13		19	21		⇨
ROW 1	1	2	4	9	10	12	17	18	20	25	⇨

The array of numbers continues.

1. What is the 30th number in Row 5? _____

2. What number in Row 1 is below the 30th number in Row 5? _____

3. How did you figure out the answer to #2?

_____

4. What number in Row 1 is below the 50th number in Row 5? _____

5. Let **P** stand for the position of a number in Row 5. Complete the equation that can be used to figure out the number in Row 1 that is below the **P** number in Row 5.

Number in Row 1 = _____

Math Problem-Solving Packets: Grade 6 © 2012 by Greenes, Findell & Cavanagh, Scholastic Teaching Resources

PROBLEM
7

What number in Row 1 is below the 10th number in Row 5?

ROW 5				11				22			⇨
ROW 4				10				21			⇨
ROW 3			6	9			17	20			⇨
ROW 2		3	5	8		14	16	19		25	⇨
ROW 1	1	2	4	7	12	13	15	18	23	24	⇨

The array of numbers continues.

1. What is the 10th number in Row 5? _____

2. What number in Row 1 is below the 10th number in Row 5? _____

3. How did you figure out the answer to #2?

   _____

4. What number in Row 1 is below the 30th number in Row 5? _____

5. Let **P** stand for the position of a number in Row 5. Complete the equation that can be used to figure out the number in Row 1 that is below the **P** number in Row 5.

   Number in Row 1 = _____

Math Problem-Solving Packets: Grade 6 © 2012 by Greenes, Findell & Cavanagh, Scholastic Teaching Resources

Ticket Please

Overview

Presented with clues in the form of relationships among costs of three different types of admission tickets, students determine the cost of each ticket. This is preparation for solving systems of equations with two or three unknowns.

Problem-Solving Strategies

- Reason deductively
- Test cases

Related Math Skill

Compute with amounts of money

Algebra Focus

- Solve equations with one or two unknowns
- Replace unknowns with their values

CCSS Correlations

6.EE.2 • 6.EE.5 • 6.EE.6 • 6.EE.7

Math Language

- Cost
- Replace
- Total cost

Introducing the Packet

Make photocopies of "Solve the Problem: Ticket Please" (page 33) and distribute to students. Have students work in pairs, encouraging them to discuss strategies they might use to solve the problem. You may want to walk around and listen in on some of their discussions. After a few minutes, display the problem on the interactive whiteboard (see the CD) and use the following questions to guide a whole-class discussion on how to solve the problem:

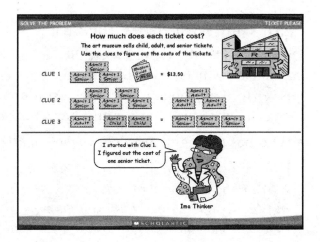

- What is the problem you have to solve? *(Figure out the cost of the tickets)*

- Look at the clues. How many different types of tickets are shown? *(3)* What are they? *(child, adult, and senior)*

- What does Clue 1 show? *(The total cost of 3 senior tickets and a museum guide is $13.50. The museum guide costs $4.50.)*

- What does Clue 2 show? *(The total cost of 5 senior tickets is the same as the total cost of 3 adult tickets.)*

- What does Clue 3 show? *(The total cost of 1 adult ticket and 2 child tickets is the same as the total cost of 3 senior tickets.)*

- Why do you think that Ima started with Clue 1? *(Since it gives information about only one type of ticket, you can figure out the cost of that ticket. The other clues give information about two or three different types of tickets.)*

- How can you figure out the cost of a senior ticket? *(Remove the museum guide and subtract $4.50 from the total cost. The 3 senior tickets cost $9.00 and each ticket is $9.00 ÷ 3, or $3.00.)*

- If you know the cost of a senior ticket, which clue can you use next to get the cost of a different ticket? *(Clue 2)* Why? *(Replace each senior ticket with its cost in Clue 2. The adult ticket is leftover. In Clue 3, if you replace each senior ticket with its cost, you still have two other tickets with unknown costs.)*

- What is the cost of an adult ticket? *($5.00)* How do you know? *(The total cost of the 5 senior tickets is 5 x $3.00, or $15.00, so each adult ticket is $15.00 ÷ 3, or $5.00.)*

- How can you figure out the cost of a child's ticket? *(Replace each adult and senior ticket with its cost. Then solve for the cost of a child's ticket.)*

Work together as a class to answer the questions in "Solve the Problem: Ticket Please."

Math Chat With "Make the Case"

Display "Make the Case: Ticket Please" on the interactive whiteboard. Before students can decide which character's "circuits are connected," they need to figure out the answer to the problem. Encourage students to work in pairs to solve the problem, then bring the class together for another whole-class discussion. Ask:

- Who has the right answer? *(Mighty Mouth)*

- How did you figure it out? *(In Clue 3, the total cost of 2 senior tickets and a $3.00 magazine is $7.00. So the 2 senior tickets are $7.00 – $3.00, or $4.00, and each is $4.00 ÷ 2, or $2.00. In Clue 1, since 2 child tickets cost the same as one senior ticket, each child ticket is $1.00. In Clue 2, replace the senior and child tickets with their costs, then 2 x $2.00 + 4 x $1.00 = 2 adult tickets; $8.00 is the cost of 2 adult tickets, so each adult ticket is $8.00 ÷ 2, or $4.00.)*

- How do you think Boodles got the answer of $2.00? *(Boodles mistakenly gave the cost of the senior ticket.)*

- How do you think CeCe Circuits got the answer of $8.00? *(She probably used the second clue and solved for the cost of the 2 adult tickets. She forgot to divide that amount by 2.)*

Name _____ Date _____

SOLVE THE PROBLEM

How much does each ticket cost?

The art museum sells child, adult, and senior tickets.
Use the clues to figure out the costs of the tickets.

CLUE 1  Admit 1 Senior, Admit 1 Senior, Admit 1 Senior Museum Guide $4.50 = $13.50

CLUE 2 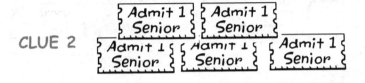 Admit 1 Senior, Admit 1 Senior, Admit 1 Senior, Admit 1 Senior, Admit 1 Senior = Admit 1 Adult, Admit 1 Adult, Admit 1 Adult

CLUE 3 Admit 1 Adult, Admit 1 Child, Admit 1 Child = Admit 1 Senior, Admit 1 Senior, Admit 1 Senior

I started with Clue **1**.
I figured out the cost of
one senior ticket.

Ima Thinker

1. A senior ticket costs $_____ .

2. An adult ticket costs $_____ .

3. A child ticket costs $_____ .

4. How did you figure out the cost of a child ticket? _____

_____

Name _____ Date _____

MAKE THE CASE

How much does an adult ticket cost?

The train station sells child, adult, and senior tickets.
Use the clues to figure out the costs of the tickets.

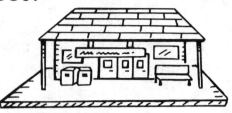

CLUE 1 [Admit 1 Child] [Admit 1 Child] **=** [Admit 1 Senior]

CLUE 2 [Admit 1 Senior] [Admit 1 Senior] [Admit 1 Child] [Admit 1 Child] **=** [Admit 1 Adult] [Admit 1 Adult]

CLUE 3 [Admit 1 Senior] [Admit 1 Senior] [Stay on Track #3.00] **= $7.00**

Boodles

No way. An adult ticket is $2.00.

That's easy. An adult ticket is $4.00.

Mighty Mouth

You are off track. An adult ticket is $8.00.

CeCe Circuits

Whose circuits are connected?

Math Problem-Solving Packets: Grade 6 © 2012 by Greenes, Findell & Cavanagh, Scholastic Teaching Resources

Name _____ Date _____

PROBLEM

1

How much does each ticket cost?

The science museum sells child, adult, and senior tickets.
Use the clues to figure out the costs of the tickets.

CLUE 1

CLUE 2

CLUE 3      = $11.00

> I started with Clue **3**.
> I figured out the cost of
> one child ticket.

Ima Thinker

1. A child ticket costs $_____ .

2. A senior ticket costs $_____ .

3. An adult ticket costs $_____ .

4. How did you figure out the cost of an adult ticket? _____

_____

Math Problem-Solving Packets: Grade 6 © 2012 by Greenes, Findell & Cavanagh, Scholastic Teaching Resources

Name _____ Date _____

PROBLEM 2

How much does each ticket cost?

The Serpentarium sells child, adult, and senior tickets. Use the clues to figure out the costs of the tickets.

CLUE 1

| Admit 1 Senior | Admit 1 Senior | = | Admit 1 Child | Admit 1 Child |

| Admit 1 Senior | | Admit 1 Child | Admit 1 Child |

CLUE 2

| Admit 1 Adult | Admit 1 Adult |  **= $17.00**

(The Book of Snakes — $5.00)

CLUE 3

| Admit 1 Senior | Admit 1 Senior | Admit 1 Senior | = | Admit 1 Adult | Admit 1 Adult |

I started with Clue **2**.
I figured out the cost of one adult ticket.

Ima Thinker

1. An adult ticket costs $_____ .

2. A senior ticket costs $_____ .

3. A child ticket costs $_____ .

4. How did you figure out the cost of a child ticket? _____

_____

Math Problem-Solving Packets: Grade 6 © 2012 by Greenes, Findell & Cavanagh, Scholastic Teaching Resources

Name _____ Date _____

PROBLEM

3   How much does each ticket cost?

The photography museum sells child, adult, and senior tickets. Use the clues to figure out the costs of the tickets.

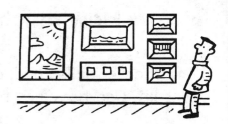

CLUE 1   [Admit 1 Senior] [Admit 1 Senior] = $11.00

CLUE 2   [Admit 1 Child] [Admit 1 Child] [Admit 1 Child]  $4.50 = [Admit 1 Senior] [Admit 1 Senior] [Admit 1 Senior]

CLUE 3   [Admit 1 Adult] [Admit 1 Adult] [Admit 1 Senior] [Admit 1 Senior] = [Admit 1 Child] [Admit 1 Child] [Admit 1 Child] [Admit 1 Child] [Admit 1 Child] [Admit 1 Child]

> I started with Clue **1**.
> I figured out the cost of
> one senior ticket.

Ima Thinker

1. A senior ticket costs $_____ .

2. A child ticket costs $_____ .

3. An adult ticket costs $_____ .

4. How did you figure out the cost of an adult ticket? _____

_____

Math Problem-Solving Packets: Grade 6 © 2012 by Greenes, Findell & Cavanagh, Scholastic Teaching Resources

Name _____ Date _____

PROBLEM 4

How much does each ticket cost?

The theater sells child, adult, and senior tickets for the rock concert. Use the clues to figure out the costs of the tickets.

CLUE 1   [Admit 1 Adult] [Admit 1 Child] [Admit 1 Child] =  $3.00   [Admit 1 Senior] [Admit 1 Senior]

CLUE 2   [Admit 1 Senior] [Admit 1 Senior] [Admit 1 Senior] [Admit 1 Senior] = [Admit 1 Adult] [Admit 1 Adult] [Admit 1 Adult]

CLUE 3   [Admit 1 Senior] [Admit 1 Senior] [Admit 1 Senior] [Admit 1 Senior]  $10.00 8 Earplugs   = $40.00

I started with Clue **3**.
I figured out the cost of one senior ticket.

Ima Thinker

1. A senior ticket costs $_____ .

2. An adult ticket costs $_____ .

3. A child ticket costs $_____ .

4. How did you figure out the cost of a child ticket? _____

_____

Math Problem-Solving Packets: Grade 6 © 2012 by Greenes, Findell & Cavanagh, Scholastic Teaching Resources

Name _____ Date _____

PROBLEM 5

How much does each ticket cost?

The aquarium sells child, adult, and senior tickets.
Use the clues to figure out the costs of the tickets.

CLUE 1   Admit 1 Adult / Admit 1 Adult **=** Admit 1 Senior / Admit 1 Senior   Admit 1 Child / Admit 1 Child

CLUE 2   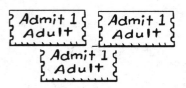   **= $30.00**

CLUE 3   Admit 1 Child / Admit 1 Child   Admit 1 Adult **= $14.00**

1. An adult ticket costs $_____ .

2. A child ticket costs $_____ .

3. A senior ticket costs $_____ .

4. How did you figure out the cost of a senior ticket? _____

_____

Math Problem-Solving Packets: Grade 6 © 2012 by Greenes, Findell & Cavanagh, Scholastic Teaching Resources

Name _____ Date _____

PROBLEM 6

How much does each ticket cost?

NOW SHOWING

The movie theater sells child, adult, and senior tickets.
Use the clues to figure out the costs of the tickets.

CLUE 1   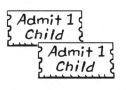       = $20.00

Admit 1 Child, Admit 1 Child, Fresh #6.25, Fresh #6.25

CLUE 2     = $30.00

Admit 1 Child, Admit 1 Senior, Admit 1 Adult, Admit 1 Adult

CLUE 3    =

Admit 1 Adult, Admit 1 Adult = Admit 1 Child, Admit 1 Child, Admit 1 Child, Admit 1 Child, $4.00

---

1. A child ticket costs $_____ .

2. An adult ticket costs $_____ .

3. A senior ticket costs $_____ .

4. How did you figure out the cost of a senior ticket? _____

_____

Math Problem-Solving Packets: Grade 6 © 2012 by Greenes, Findell & Cavanagh, Scholastic Teaching Resources

Name _____ Date _____

PROBLEM 7

How much does each ticket cost?

The double-decker tour bus sells child, adult, and senior tickets. Use the clues to figure out the costs of the tickets.

CLUE 1 | Admit 1 Adult | | Admit 1 Senior | **=** | Admit 1 Child | | Admit 1 Child | | Admit 1 Child |

CLUE 2 | Admit 1 Adult | | Admit 1 Adult | | Admit 1 Senior | | Admit 1 Senior | **= $30.00**

CLUE 3 | Admit 1 Senior | | Admit 1 Senior | $7.50 $8.00   **= $28.00**

1. A senior ticket costs $_____ .

2. An adult ticket costs $_____ .

3. A child ticket costs $_____ .

4. How did you figure out the cost of a child ticket? _____

_____

Blocky Balance

Overview

Presented with clues about the relative weights of three different types of blocks in a pan balance, students figure out which blocks will balance a new set of blocks.

Problem-Solving Strategies

- Reason about proportional relationships
- Reason deductively

Related Math Skill

Compute with whole numbers

Algebra Focus

- Understand that substituting one set of blocks with a second set of equal weight preserves balance
- Explore the concept of equality
- Understand that multiplying or dividing the number of objects on both sides of a two-pan balance by the same number preserves balance
- Replace unknowns with their values

CCSS Correlations

6.RP.2 • 6.RP.3d • 6.EE.5 6.EE.7

Math Language

- Balance
- Substitute

Introducing the Packet

Make photocopies of "Solve the Problem: Blocky Balance" (page 44) and distribute to students. Have students work in pairs, encouraging them to discuss strategies they might use to solve the problem. You may want to walk around and listen in on some of their discussions. After a few minutes, display the problem on the interactive whiteboard (see the CD) and use the following questions to guide a whole-class discussion on how to solve the problem:

- Look at the first pan balance. What do the pans show? *(4 spheres in one pan balancing 2 cylinders in the other pan)* In the second pan balance, what do the pans show? *(6 cylinders balancing 4 cubes)*

- What does it mean that two pans are balanced? *(The total weight of the blocks in each pan is the same.)*

- What do you need to find out? *(How many cubes will balance 12 spheres)*

- How many spheres will balance 1 cylinder? *(2)* And 4 cylinders? *(8)* And 6 cylinders? *(12)*

- Why did Ima start with the first pan balance? *(She could figure out that the weight of 1 cylinder equals, or balances, 2 spheres.)*

- In the second pan balance, if you substitute 2 spheres for each cylinder, how many spheres will be in the pan on the left? *(12)*

Work together as a class to answer the questions in "Solve the Problem: Blocky Balance."

Math Chat With "Make the Case"

Display "Make the Case: Blocky Balance" on the interactive whiteboard. Before students can decide which character's "circuits are connected," they need to figure out the answer to the problem. Encourage students to work in pairs to solve the problem, then bring the class together for another whole-class discussion. Ask:

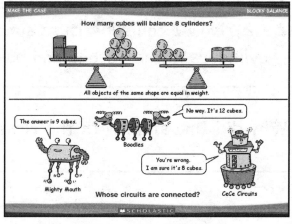

- Who has the right answer? *(CeCe Circuits)*

- How did you figure it out? *(In the first pan balance, 3 cubes balance 6 spheres. So, 1 cube (3 ÷ 3) balances 2 spheres (6 ÷ 3). In the second pan balance, substitute 1 cube for every 2 spheres. Then 2 cubes balance 2 cylinders. So, 8 cubes (4 x 2) will balance 8 cylinders (4 x 2).)*

- How do you think Boodles got the answer 12? *(Boodles may have multiplied both the number of cylinders and the number of cubes shown by 4. So, in the second pan balance, Boodles multiplied the 2 cylinders by 4 to get 8 cylinders, and then multiplied the 3 cubes in the first pan balance by 4 to get 12 cubes.)*

- How do you think Mighty Mouth got the answer of 9 cubes? *(He may have added 6 cylinders to the cylinders in the second pan balance to get 8 cylinders, and likewise added the 6 cubes to the number of cubes in the first pan balance to get 9 cubes.)*

SOLVE THE PROBLEM

How many cubes will balance 12 spheres?

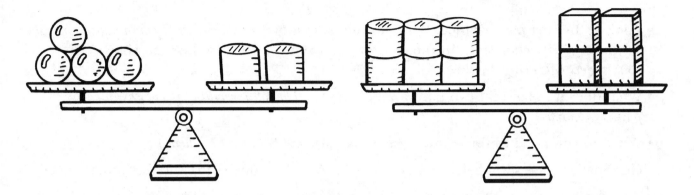

All objects of the same shape are equal in weight.

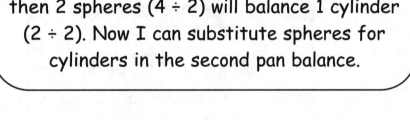

I'll start with the first pan balance. Since 4 spheres weigh the same as 2 cylinders, then 2 spheres (4 ÷ 2) will balance 1 cylinder (2 ÷ 2). Now I can substitute spheres for cylinders in the second pan balance.

Ima Thinker

1. Why did Ima start with the first pan balance?

_____

_____

2. How many cubes balance 12 spheres? _____

3. How did you figure it out? _____

_____

4. If 1 cylinder weighs 12 pounds, what's the weight of 1 sphere? _____

5. If 1 cube weighs 6 pounds, what's the weight of 1 sphere? _____

Name _____ Date _____

MAKE THE CASE

How many cubes will balance 8 cylinders?

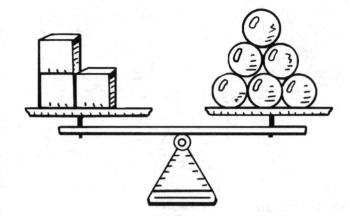
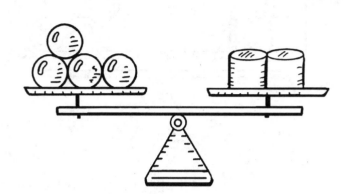

All objects of the same shape are equal in weight.

Boodles

No way.
It's 12 cubes.

The answer is
9 cubes.

Mighty Mouth

You're wrong.
I am sure
it's 8 cubes.

CeCe Circuits

Whose circuits are connected?

Name _____ Date _____

PROBLEM 1

How many cylinders will balance 3 cubes?

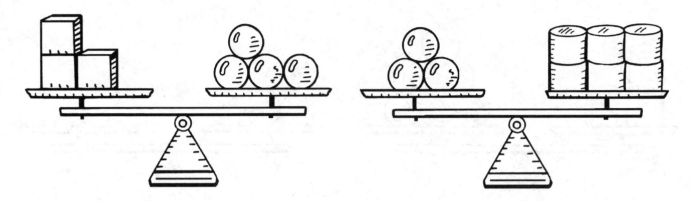

All objects of the same shape are equal in weight.

I'll start with the second pan balance. Since 3 spheres weigh the same as 6 cylinders, then 1 sphere (3 ÷ 3) will balance 2 cylinders (6 ÷ 3). Now I can substitute cylinders for spheres in the first pan balance.

Ima Thinker

1. Why did Ima start with the second pan balance?

   _____

   _____

2. How many cylinders will balance 3 cubes? _____

3. How did you figure it out? _____

   _____

4. If 1 sphere weighs 6 pounds, what's the weight of 1 cube? _____

5. If 1 sphere weighs 6 pounds, what's the weight of 1 cylinder? _____

Name _____   Date _____

PROBLEM 2

How many cubes will balance 2 spheres?

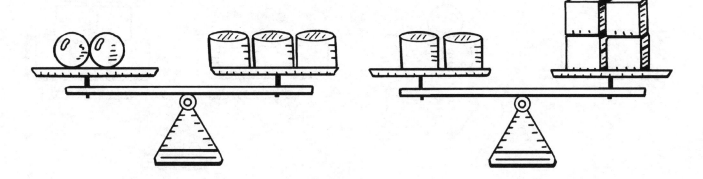

All objects of the same shape are equal in weight.

I'll start with the second pan balance. Since 2 cylinders weigh the same as 4 cubes, then 1 cylinder (2 ÷ 2) will balance 2 cubes (4 ÷ 2). Now I can substitute cubes for cylinders in the first pan balance.

1. Why did Ima start with the second pan balance and then find the number of cubes that balance 3 cylinders? _____

   _____

Ima Thinker

2. How many cubes will balance 2 spheres? _____

3. How did you figure it out? _____

   _____

4. If 1 cylinder weighs 12 pounds, what's the weight of 1 sphere? _____

5. If 1 sphere weighs 12 pounds, what's the weight of 1 cube? _____

PROBLEM 3

How many spheres will balance 6 cylinders?

All objects of the same shape are equal in weight.

I'll start with the first pan balance. Since 2 cubes weigh the same as 4 spheres, then 1 cube (2 ÷ 2) will balance 2 spheres (4 ÷ 2). Now I can substitute spheres for cubes in the second pan balance.

Ima Thinker

1. Why did Ima start with the first pan balance?

   _____

   _____

2. How many spheres will balance 3 cylinders? _____

3. How many spheres will balance 6 cylinders? _____

4. How did you figure out the answer to #3? _____

   _____

5. If 1 sphere weighs 3 pounds, what's the weight of 1 cylinder? _____

Math Problem-Solving Packets: Grade 6 © 2012 by Greenes, Findell & Cavanagh, Scholastic Teaching Resources

Name _____ Date _____

PROBLEM 4

How many cubes will balance 4 spheres?

All objects of the same shape are equal in weight.

1. How many cubes will balance 1 cylinder? _____

2. How many cubes will balance 2 spheres? _____

3. How many cubes will balance 4 spheres? _____

4. How did you figure out the answer to #3? _____

_____

5. If 1 sphere weighs 15 pounds, what's the weight of 1 cube? _____

Name _____ Date _____

PROBLEM 5

How many cubes will balance 9 cylinders?

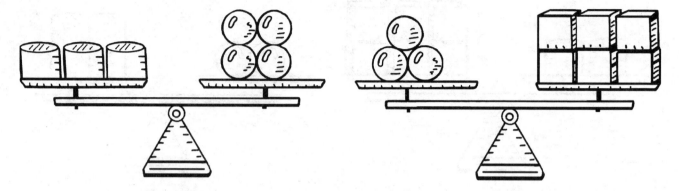

All objects of the same shape are equal in weight.

1. How many cubes will balance 1 sphere? _____

2. How many cubes will balance 3 cylinders? _____

3. How many cubes will balance 9 cylinders? _____

4. How did you figure out the answer to #3? _____

_____

5. If 1 cube weighs 6 pounds, what's the weight of 1 cylinder? _____

Name _____ Date _____

PROBLEM 6

How many cubes will balance 12 cylinders?

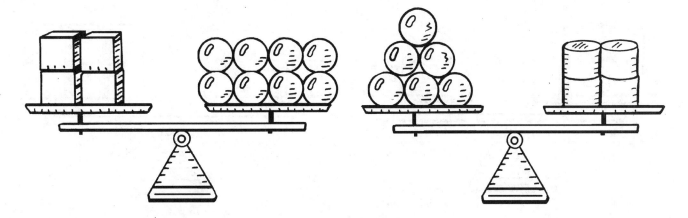

All objects of the same shape are equal in weight.

1. How many spheres will balance 1 cube? _____

2. How many cubes will balance 4 cylinders? _____

3. How many cubes will balance 12 cylinders? _____

4. How did you figure out the answer to #3? _____

_____

5. If 1 cylinder weighs 9 pounds, what's the weight of 1 cube? _____

Name _____ Date _____

PROBLEM 7

How many spheres will balance 6 cylinders?

All objects of the same shape are equal in weight.

1. How many cubes will balance 1 cylinder? _____

2. How many cylinders will balance 5 spheres? _____

3. How many spheres will balance 6 cylinders? _____

4. How did you figure out the answer to #3? _____

_____

5. If 1 sphere weighs 8 pounds, what's the weight of 1 cylinder? _____

Math Problem-Solving Packets: Grade 6 © 2012 by Greenes, Findell & Cavanagh, Scholastic Teaching Resources

In Good Shape

Overview

Students interpret mathematical relationships, apply area and perimeter formulas, and work backward through clues to figure out perimeters and areas of rectangles.

Problem-Solving Strategies

- Work backward
- Use logical reasoning

Related Math Skills

- Compute perimeters of rectangles ($P = l + l + w + w$ or $P = 2l + 2w$)
- Compute the areas of rectangles ($A = l \times w$)
- Recognize that opposite sides of rectangles are the same length
- Understand that squares are rectangles

Algebra Focus

- Represent quantitative relationships with symbols
- Write and solve equations (formulas)

CCSS Correlations

6.EE.2 • 6.EE.3 • 6.EE.4 • 6.EE.5
6.EE.6 • 6.EE.7 • 6.G.1

Math Language

- Area
- Perimeter
- Width
- Length
- Twice
- Half
- One-fifth
- One-fourth
- One-third
- Rectangle
- Square

Introducing the Packet

Make photocopies of "Solve the Problem: In Good Shape" (page 55) and distribute to students. Have students work in pairs, encouraging them to discuss strategies they might use to solve the problem. You may want to walk around and listen in on some of their discussions. After a few minutes, display the problem on the interactive whiteboard (see the CD) and use the following questions to guide a whole-class discussion on how to solve the problem:

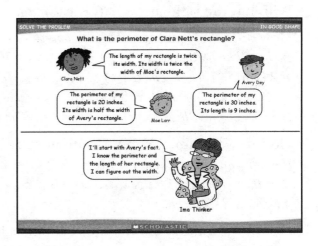

- How can you figure out the perimeter of a rectangle? *(Add the lengths of its sides.)*

- What do you know about the lengths of opposite sides of a rectangle? *(They are the same length.)*

- Suppose that the length of a rectangle is 3 inches and its width is 5 inches, what is its perimeter? *(3 + 3 + 5 + 5, or 16 inches)*

- Why can't you start with Clara's fact? *(To figure out the length of her rectangle, you have to know the width. You don't know the width since it is related to the width of Moe's rectangle.)*

- Why can't you start with Moe's fact? *(To figure out the width of his rectangle, you have to know the width of Avery's rectangle.)*

- How can you figure out the width of Avery's rectangle? *(The perimeter is l + l + w + w. So, 30 = 9 + 9 + w + w and 12 = w + w. The width of Avery's rectangle is 12 ÷ 2, or 6 inches.)*

- What is the width of Moe's rectangle? *(6 ÷ 2, or 3 inches)*

- What is the length of Moe's rectangle? *(20 = l + l + 3 + 3, and 14 = l + l. So, l = 14 ÷ 2, or 7 inches.)*

- What's the length of Clara's rectangle? *(2 x 6, or 12 inches)*

- What is the width of Clara's rectangle? *(2 x 3, or 6 inches)*

Work together as a class to answer the questions in "Solve the Problem: In Good Shape."

Math Chat With "Make the Case"

Display "Make the Case: In Good Shape" on the interactive whiteboard. Before students can decide which character's "circuits are connected," they need to figure out the answer to the problem. Encourage students to work in pairs to solve the problem, then bring the class together for another whole-class discussion. Ask:

- Who has the right answer? *(CeCe Circuits)*

- How did you figure it out? *(The length of Hugo's rectangle is 9 inches and the width is 6 inches. The perimeter is (2 x 9) + (2 x 6), or 30 inches. The perimeter of Justin's rectangle is 30 + 24, or 54 inches. The length is 17 inches. To figure out the width: 54 = 17 + 17 + w + w, so 20 = w + w. The width is 20 ÷ 2, or 10 inches. The length of Paige's rectangle is 2 x 17, or 34 inches. The width is 2 x 10, or 20 inches. The perimeter is (2 x 34) + (2 x 20), or 108 inches.)*

- How do you think Mighty Mouth got 216 inches for the perimeter? *(He may have thought that since Paige's rectangle is 2 times as long and 2 times as wide as Justin's rectangle, that the perimeter of Paige's rectangle is 2 x 2, or 4 times the perimeter of Justin's rectangle; 4 x 54 is 216 inches.)*

- How do you think Boodles got 54 inches for the perimeter? *(Boodles may have added 20 and 34, not remembering that a rectangle has 4 sides.)*

Name _____ Date _____

SOLVE THE PROBLEM

What is the perimeter of Clara Nett's rectangle?

Clara Nett

The length of my rectangle is twice its width. Its width is twice the width of Moe's rectangle.

Avery Dey

The perimeter of my rectangle is 20 inches. Its width is half the width of Avery's rectangle.

Moe Larr

The perimeter of my rectangle is 30 inches. Its length is 9 inches.

I'll start with Avery's fact. I know the perimeter and the length of her rectangle. I can figure out the width.

Ima Thinker

1. Why did Ima start with Avery's fact?

_____

_____

2. What is the width of Moe's rectangle? _____

3. What is the length of Moe's rectangle? _____

4. What is the width of Clara's rectangle? _____

5. How did you figure out the perimeter of Clara's rectangle?

_____

_____

MAKE THE CASE

What is the perimeter of Paige Turner's rectangle?

Paige Turner

The length of my rectangle is twice the length of Justin's rectangle. The width of my rectangle is twice the width of Justin's rectangle.

Hugo First

The perimeter of my rectangle is 24 inches greater than the perimeter of Hugo's rectangle. The length of my rectangle is 17 inches.

Justin Time

The length of my rectangle is 3 inches more than its width. Its width is 6 inches.

Boodles

You're both wrong. The perimeter is 54 inches.

I have no doubt. The perimeter is 216 inches.

Mighty Mouth

I am certain that the perimeter of Paige Turner's rectangle is 108 inches.

CeCe Circuits

Whose circuits are connected?

Math Problem-Solving Packets: Grade 6 © 2012 by Greenes, Findell & Cavanagh, Scholastic Teaching Resources

PROBLEM 1

What is the perimeter of Mac O'Roaney's rectangle?

Mac O'Roaney

My rectangle is 3 inches wider than Earl's rectangle. The length of my rectangle is 3 times its width.

Polly Ester

The perimeter of my rectangle is half the perimeter of Polly's square. The width of my rectangle is 4 inches.

Earl E. Byrd

My square has a perimeter of 36 inches.

I'll start with Polly's fact. I can figure out the length of each side of her square.

Ima Thinker

1. Why did Ima start with Polly's fact first?

_____

_____

2. What is the length of Earl's rectangle? _____

3. What is the length and width of Mac's rectangle? _____

4. How did you figure out the perimeter of Mac's rectangle?

_____

_____

Name _____ Date _____

PROBLEM 2

What is the perimeter of Ira Peete's rectangle?

Ira Peete

The width of my rectangle is ¼ the width of Joe's rectangle. My rectangle has an area of 24 square inches.

Ella Funt

My rectangle is half as long and twice as wide as Ella's rectangle.

Joe King

My rectangle is 6 inches long. Its area is 48 square inches.

I'll start with Ella's fact. I can figure out the width of her rectangle.

Ima Thinker

1. Which fact did Ima use first?

   _____

   _____

2. What is the perimeter of Ella's rectangle? _____

3. What is the perimeter of Joe's rectangle? _____

4. How did you figure out the perimeter of Ira's rectangle?

   _____

   _____

Math Problem-Solving Packets: Grade 6 © © 2012 by Greenes, Findell & Cavanagh, Scholastic Teaching Resources

Name _____ Date _____

PROBLEM 3

What is the area of Minnie Vann's rectangle?

Minnie Vann

The width of my rectangle is ½ the width of Isadora's rectangle. The perimeter of my rectangle is 22 inches.

Justin Case

My rectangle has half the area of Justin's rectangle. The length of my rectangle is half the length of Justin's square.

Isadora Bell

The area of my square is 64 square inches.

I'll start with Justin's fact. I can figure out the length of each side of his square.

Ima Thinker

1. Why did Ima start with Justin's fact first?

_____

_____

2. What is the width of Isadora's rectangle? _____

3. What is the length of Minnie's rectangle? _____

4. How did you figure out the area of Minnie's rectangle?

_____

_____

IN GOOD SHAPE

What is the area of Ray Dio's rectangle?

Ray Dio

The length of my rectangle is $\frac{1}{2}$ the width of Uriel's rectangle. The width of my rectangle is $\frac{1}{2}$ its length.

The length of my rectangle is 4 times its width. Its width is 4 inches.

Pete Zaria

The width of my rectangle is $\frac{1}{2}$ the length of Dee's rectangle. The area of my rectangle is 32 square inches.

Uriel Smart

Dee Zember

The length of my rectangle is $\frac{1}{2}$ the length of Pete's rectangle. The area of my rectangle is 16 square inches.

I'll start with Pete's fact. I can figure out the length of his rectangle.

Ima Thinker

1. Why did Ima start with Pete's fact first?

   _____

   _____

2. What is the length of Dee's rectangle? _____

3. What is the width of Uriel's rectangle? _____

4. What is the area of Ray's rectangle? How did you figure it out?

   _____

   _____

Math Problem-Solving Packets: Grade 6 © 2012 by Greenes, Findell & Cavanagh, Scholastic Teaching Resources

Name _____ Date _____

PROBLEM 5

What is the width and perimeter of Jack Kuzi's rectangle?

Jack Kuzi

The length of my rectangle is 3 times its width. Its width is 2 inches less than the width of Sarah's rectangle.

The width of my rectangle is $\frac{1}{3}$ the length of Shelley's rectangle. Its area is 40 square inches.

Sarah Nade

The width of my rectangle is $\frac{1}{4}$ the length of Tim's rectangle. The area of my rectangle is 24 square inches.

Shelley Shore

Tim Burr

The width of my rectangle is 5 inches. Its perimeter is 26 inches.

1. What is the area of Tim's rectangle? _____

2. What is the perimeter of Shelley's rectangle? _____

3. What is the perimeter of Sarah's rectangle? _____

4. What is the width and perimeter of Jack Kuzi's rectangle? _____

5. How did you figure out the width and perimeter of Jack Kuzi's rectangle? _____

_____

Name _____ Date _____

What is the perimeter of Tamara Knight's rectangle?

Tamara Knight

The area of my rectangle is 6 square inches more than the area of Lon's rectangle. Its width is one more than 3 times the width of Lon's rectangle.

The length of my rectangle is 2 inches greater than its width. The area of my rectangle is 24 square inches.

Dorie Sajar

My rectangle has an area of 22 square inches. Its width is $\frac{1}{3}$ the width of May's rectangle.

Lon Moore

May O'Nays

The length of my rectangle is $\frac{1}{3}$ the length of Dorie's rectangle. The perimeter of my rectangle is 16 inches.

1. What is the perimeter of Dorie's rectangle? _____

2. What is the area of May's rectangle? _____

3. What is the perimeter of Lon's rectangle? _____

4. What is the perimeter of Tamara's rectangle? _____

5. How did you figure out the perimeter of Tamara's rectangle?

_____

_____

Math Problem-Solving Packets: Grade 6 © 2012 by Greenes, Findell & Cavanagh, Scholastic Teaching Resources

Name _____ Date _____

PROBLEM
7

What is the perimeter of Rhoda and Rita Booke's rectangle?

Rhoda and Rita Booke

Our rectangle has $\frac{1}{4}$ the area of Tom's rectangle. The length of our rectangle is 1 inch greater than its width.

The length of my rectangle is twice the length of Parker's rectangle. Its perimeter is 32 inches.

Tom Morro

The length of my rectangle is $\frac{1}{5}$ the length of Alex's rectangle. The perimeter of my rectangle is the same as her rectangle.

Parker Carr

Alex Blaine

The area of my rectangle is 50 square inches. Its width is half its length.

1. What is the perimeter of Alex's rectangle? _____

2. What is the area of Parker's rectangle? _____

3. What is the area of Tom's rectangle? ___   ___

4. What is the perimeter of Rhoda and Rita's rectangle? _____

5. How did you figure out the perimeter of Rhoda and Rita's rectangle?

_____

_____

Numbaglyphics

Overview

Presented with various letters that represent numbers, students use the column sums to figure out the value of each symbol.

Problem-Solving Strategies
- Reason deductively
- Reason proportionally
- Test cases

Related Math Skill

Compute with whole numbers

Algebra Focus
- Solve equations with three unknowns
- Replace unknowns with their values
- Recognize that same symbols have the same value
- Understand that taking away an addend changes the sum by the same amount

CCSS Correlations

6.EE.2 • 6.EE.3 • 6.EE.4 • 6.EE.5
6.EE.6 • 6.EE.7

Math Language
- Decipher
- Replace
- Symbol
- Value

Introducing the Packet

Make photocopies of "Solve the Problem: Numbaglyphics" (page 66) and distribute to students. Have students work in pairs, encouraging them to discuss strategies they might use to solve the problem. You may want to walk around and listen in on some of their discussions. After a few minutes, display the problem on the interactive whiteboard (see the CD) and use the following questions to guide a whole-class discussion on how to solve the problem:

- What is in the cube? (*Three columns of numbers and symbols*)

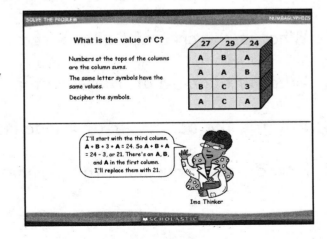

- What are the numbers at the tops of the columns? *(Sums of the numbers and the values of the symbols in the columns)*

- How many different symbols are there? *(Three)*

- How are the columns alike? *(They all have an A and a B.)*

- How are they different? *(The third column contains the number 3, and the second column is the only column that contains the letter C.)*

- Why did Ima start with the third column? *(You can remove 3 from the column and the sum of A + B + A is 24 − 3, or 21.)*

- When you replace A + B + A with 21 in the first column, what is the value of the extra A? *(27 − 21, or 6.)*

- How can you figure out the value of B? *(In the first or third columns, replace each A with 6. Then solve for the value of B, which is 9.)*

- How can you figure out the value of C? *(In the second column, replace A with its value of 6 and B with its value of 9. Then the sum C + C is 29 − 9 − 6, or 14, and C = 14 ÷ 2, or 7.)*

Math Chat With "Make the Case"

Display "Make the Case: Numbaglyphics" on the interactive whiteboard. Before students can decide which character's "circuits are connected," they need to figure out the answer to the problem. Encourage students to work in pairs to solve the problem, then bring the class together for another whole-class discussion. Ask:

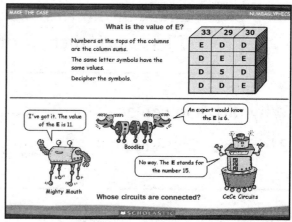

- Who has the right answer? *(Boodles)*

- How did you figure it out? *(In the second column, D + E + D = 29 − 5, or 24. In the first column, replace the D, E, and D with 24. Then the extra D is 33 − 24, or 9. In the first column, replace each D with 9. Then E = 33 − 9 − 9 − 9, or 6.)*

- Why do you think Mighty Mouth answered 11? *(He probably saw three Ds in the first column and thought that 33 ÷ 3 would give the value for E.)*

- How do you think CeCe Circuits got the answer 15? *(She mistakenly added the values of D and E. In the third column, she may have also replaced D and E with 15 and then subtracted 15 from 30 to get 15.)*

Name _____ Date _____

SOLVE THE PROBLEM

What is the value of C?

Numbers at the tops of the columns are the column sums.

The same letter symbols have the same values.

Decipher the symbols.

27	29	24
A	B	A
A	A	B
B	C	3
A	C	A

I'll start with the third column. **A** + **B** + 3 + **A** = 24. So **A** + **B** + **A** = 24 – 3, or 21. There's an **A**, **B**, and **A** in the first column. I'll replace them with 21.

Ima Thinker

1. Why did Ima replace the **A**, **B**, and **A** with 21 in the first column? _____

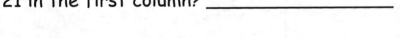

2. What is the value of **B**? _____

3. What is the value of **C**? _____

4. How did you figure out the answer to #3? _____

_____

5. What is the value of **A** + **A** + **A** + **B** + **B** + **C** + **C**? _____

Math Problem-Solving Packets: Grade 6 © 2012 by Greenes, Findell & Cavanagh, Scholastic Teaching Resources

Name _____ Date _____

MAKE THE CASE

What is the value of E?

Numbers at the tops of the columns are the column sums.

The same letter symbols have the same values.

Decipher the symbols.

33	29	30
E	D	D
D	E	E
D	5	D
D	D	E

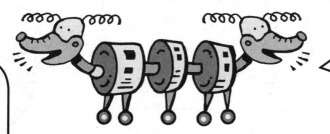

Boodles

An expert would know that **E** is 6.

I've got it. The value of the **E** is 11.

Mighty Mouth

No way. The **E** stands for the number 15.

CeCe Circuits

Whose circuits are connected?

PROBLEM 1

What is the value of F?

Numbers at the tops of the columns are the column sums.

The same letter symbols have the same values.

Decipher the symbols.

13	19	23
F	4	G
F	G	G
F	F	F
G	6	G

I'll start with the second column. 4 + **G** + F + 6 = 19. So, **G** + **F** = 9. There's a **G** and **F** in the first column. I'll replace them with 9.

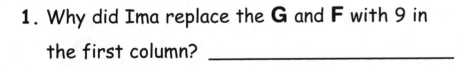

Ima Thinker

1. Why did Ima replace the **G** and **F** with 9 in the first column? _____

   _____

2. What is the value of **G**? _____

3. How did you figure out the value of **G**? _____

   _____

4. **F + G + G + G** = _____

5. How many **F** are equal in value to **G + G**? _____

Math Problem-Solving Packets: Grade 6 © 2012 by Greenes, Findell & Cavanagh, Scholastic Teaching Resources

PROBLEM 2

What is the value of J?

Numbers at the tops of the columns are the column sums.

The same letter symbols have the same values.

Decipher the symbols.

19	12	13
H	I	I
I	H	I
H	I	I
J	2	H

I'll start with the second column. **I** + **H** + **I** + 2 = 12. So, **I** + **H** + **I** = 10. There's an **I**, **H**, and an **I** in the third column, I'll replace them with 10.

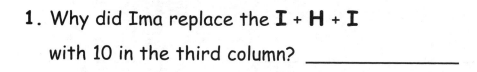

Ima Thinker

1. Why did Ima replace the **I** + **H** + **I** with 10 in the third column? _____
_____

2. What is the value of **H**? _____

3. What is the value of **J**? _____

4. How did you figure out the value of **J**? _____
_____

5. How many **H** are equal in value to **J** + **J** + **J**? _____

PROBLEM 3

What is the value of K?

Numbers at the tops of the columns are the column sums.

The same letter symbols have the same values.

Decipher the symbols.

30	22	26
M	M	M
7	K	L
L	M	M
L	L	L

> I'll start with the first column. **M** + 7 + **L** + **L** = 30. So, **M** + **L** + **L** = 23. There is an **M**, **L**, and **L** in the third column. I'll replace them with 23.

Ima Thinker

1. Why did Ima replace the **M** + **L** + **L** with 23 in the third column? _____
_____

2. What is the value of **L**? _____

3. What is the value of **K**? _____

4. How did you figure out the value of **K**? _____
_____

5. How many **K** have the same value as 10 **M**? _____

Math Problem-Solving Packets: Grade 6 © 2012 by Greenes, Findell & Cavanagh, Scholastic Teaching Resources

PROBLEM 4

What is the value of each letter?

Numbers at the tops of the columns are the column sums.

The same letter symbols have the same values.

Decipher the symbols.

34	35	32
N	O	4
O	N	N
N	P	P
O	P	P

1. What is the value of **O**? _____

2. What is the value of **N**? _____

3. What is the value of **P**? _____

4. How did you figure out the values of the symbols? _____

_____

5. How many **P** are equal in value to 9 **O**? _____

PROBLEM
5

What is the value of each letter?

Numbers at the tops of the columns are the column sums.

The same letter symbols have the same values.

Decipher the symbols.

40	46	41
R	Q	S
9	R	S
Q	Q	S
Q	R	Q

1. What is the value of **R**? _____

2. What is the value of **Q**? _____

3. What is the value of **S**? _____

4. How did you figure out the values of the symbols? _____

_____

5. How many **Q** are equal in value to 8 **R**? _____

Math Problem-Solving Packets: Grade 6 © 2012 by Greenes, Findell & Cavanagh, Scholastic Teaching Resources

PROBLEM 6

What is the value of each letter?

Numbers at the tops of the columns are the column sums.

The same letter symbols have the same values.

Decipher the symbols.

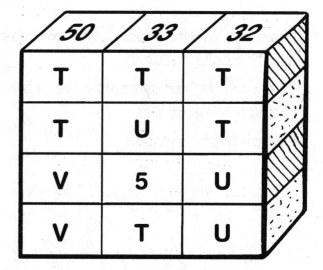

1. What is the value of **U**? _____

2. What is the value of **T**? _____

3. What is the value of **V**? _____

4. How did you figure out the values of the symbols? _____

_____

5. How many **T** are equal in value to 15 **U**? _____

PROBLEM 7

What is the value of each letter?

Numbers at the tops of the columns are the column sums.

The same letter symbols have the same values.

Decipher the symbols.

37	46	36
W	X	17
X	W	Y
Y	W	W
W	X	W

1. What is the value of **X**? _____

2. What is the value of **W**? _____

3. What is the value of **Y**? _____

4. How did you figure out the values of the symbols? _____

_____

5. How many **X** are equal in value to 40 **Y**? _____

Math Problem-Solving Packets: Grade 6 © 2012 by Greenes, Findell & Cavanagh, Scholastic Teaching Resources

SOLVE
IT

1. Look   What is the problem?

2. Plan and Do   What will you do first? How will you solve the problem?

3. Answer and Check   How can you be sure your answer is correct?

Complete the year of the invention.

The automatic teller machine (ATM) was invented
in the United States by Don Wetzel in 19___.
The letter **K** stands for a 2-digit number.
Use the clues to figure out the value of **K**.

CLUES:

1) The difference between the digits of **K** is
   greater than 2.

2) $100 \div 2 \leq K$

3) The sum of the digits of **K** is greater than 11.

4) **K** is a multiple of 3.

5) $K < 150 \div 2$.

SOLVE IT: PERPLEXING PATTERNS

What number in Row 1 is below
the 21st number in Row 4?

The array of numbers continues.

ROW 4			12			24			36	⇨
ROW 3	5	8	11	17	20	23	29	32	35	⇨
ROW 2	2	4	7	10	14	16	19	22	26	28	31	34	38	⇨
ROW 1	1	3	6	9	13	15	18	21	25	27	30	33	37	⇨

How much does each ticket cost?

The cactus garden sells child, adult, and senior tickets. Use the clues to figure out the costs of the tickets.

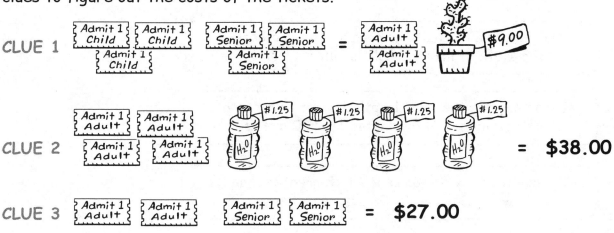

CLUE 1

CLUE 2   = $38.00

CLUE 3   = $27.00

SOLVE IT: BLOCKY BALANCE

How many cylinders will balance 10 cubes?

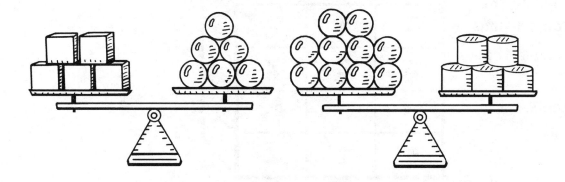

All objects of the same shape are equal in weight.

SOLVE IT: IN GOOD SHAPE

What is the perimeter of Carmen Gogh's rectangle?

Carmen Gogh

My rectangle has an area of 72 square inches. The length of my rectangle is 3 times the length of Bill's rectangle.

Bill Ding

My rectangle has half the area of Jo's rectangle. The width of my rectangle is half its length.

Jo Kerr

My rectangle is the same length as Sonny's rectangle. The perimeter of my rectangle is 20 inches.

Sonny Burns

The length of my rectangle is 1 inch greater than its width. Its area is 56 square inches.

SOLVE IT: NUMBAGLYPHICS

What is the value of $?

Numbers at the tops of the columns are the column sums.

The same symbols have the same values.

Decipher the symbols.

62	56	58
Z	%	%
%	Z	Z
21	Z	%
$	$	Z

ANSWER KEY

Inventions (pages 11–19)
Solve the Problem
1. 30, 31, 32, ..., and 49 **2.** 43 **3.** From Clues 1 and 3, A is 30, 31, 32, ..., or 49. Clue 4 eliminates all numbers except for 31, 37, 41, 43, and 47. Clue 2 eliminates 31 and 37 leaving 41, 43, and 47. Clue 5 eliminates 41 and 47. A is 43. **4.** Clue 1: 43 ≥ 30. Clue 2: 4 x 3 = 12, which is an even number. Clue 3: 43 + 43 = 86 and 86 < 100. Clue 4: The only factors of 43 are 1 and 43. Clue 5: 4 – 3 = 1 and 1 < 3. **5.** 1943

Make the Case
Whose circuits are connected?
Mighty Mouth

Problem 1
1. 16, 24, 32, ..., and 80 **2.** 80 **3.** From Clues 1 and 2, C is 16, 24, 32, ..., or 80. Clue 3 eliminates all numbers except for 40 and 80. Clue 4 eliminates 40. C is 80. **4.** Replace C with 80. Clue 1: 80 is a multiple of 8 because 10 x 8 = 80. Clue 2: 80 < 88. Clue 3: 8 x 0 = 0. Clue 4: 80 ≠ 40. **5.** 1980

Problem 2
1. 64, 65, 66, ..., and 75 **2.** 74 **3.** From Clues 2 and 3, D is 64, 65, 66, ..., or 75. Clue 1 eliminates all odd numbers, leaving 64, 66, 68, 70, 72, and 74. Clue 4 eliminates all numbers except for 70, 72, and 74. Clue 5 eliminates 70 and 72. D is 74. **4.** Replace D with 74. Clue 1: 74 is an even number. Clue 2: 74 ≤ 75. Clue 3: 74 > 63. Clue 4: 7 – 4 = 3, and 3 > 2. Clue 5: 7 x 4, or 28 > 20. **5.** 1974

Problem 3
1. 55, 56, 57, ..., and 80 **2.** 72 **3.** From Clues 2 and 3, the value of E is 55, 56, 57, ..., or 80. Clue 1 eliminates all numbers except for 60, 66, 72, and 78. Clue 4 eliminates all numbers except for 72. E is 72. **4.** Replace E with 72. Clue 1: 6 is a factor of 72 because 12 x 6 = 72. Clue 2: 72 ≠ 80. Clue 3: 72 > 54. Clue 4: 8 is a factor of 72 because 9 x 8 = 72. **5.** 1972

Problem 4
1. Clue 1 gives the greatest value possible for F: 81. Clue 4 gives the least value: 51. **2.** 79 **3.** From Clues 1 and 4, the value of F is 51, 52, 53, ..., or 81. Clue 2 eliminates all numbers except for 59, 69, and 79. Clue 3 eliminates 69. Clue 5 eliminates 59. F is 79. **4.** Replace F with 79. Clue 1: 79 ≤ 81. Clue 2: 79 ÷ 10 = 7 R 9. Clue 3: 7 + 9 = 16, which is even. Clue 4: 2 x 79 is 158 and 158 > 100. Clue 5: 79 ≠ 59. **5.** 1979

Problem 5
1. Clue 4, gives the greatest value possible for G: 99. From Clue 1, G must be 11, 22, 33, ..., or 99. **2.** 88 **3.** From Clues 1 and 4, the value of G is 11, 22, 33, 44, 55, 66, 77, 88, or 99. Clue 2 eliminates all numbers except for 22, 44, 66, and 88. Clue 3 eliminates 44 and 66. Clue 5 eliminates 22. G is 88. **4.** Replace G with 88. Clue 1: 88 is a multiple of 11. Clue 2: 2 is a factor of 88. Clue 3: 88 ÷ 3 has a remainder of 1. Clue 4: 100 > 88. Clue 5: 88 ÷ 5 has a remainder of 3. **5.** 1888

Problem 6
1. Clue 2 gives the greatest value for H: 29. Clue 4 gives the least value for H: 20. **2.** 28 **3.** From Clues 2 and 4, H can be 20, 21, 22, ..., or 29. Clue 1 eliminates all numbers except for 20, 24, and 28. Clue 3 eliminates 24. Clue 5 eliminates 20. H is 28. **4.** Replace H with 28. Clue 1: 28 is a multiple of 4 because 7 x 4 = 28. Clue 2: 60 > 56. Clue 3: 28 ÷ 3 = 9 R 1. Clue 4: 42 ≥ 30. Clue 5: 28 ≠ 20 **5.** 1928

Problem 7
1. Clue 1 gives the greatest value of J: 95. Clue 5 gives the least value for J: 20. **2.** 63 **3.** From Clues 1 and 5, J is 20, 21, 22, ..., or 95. Clue 2 indicates that J is a multiple of 3 x 7, or 21. The multiples of 21 from 20 through 95 are 21, 42, 63, and 84. Clue 3 eliminates 42 and 84 leaving 21 and 63. Clue 4 eliminates 21. J is 63. **4.** Replace J with 63. Clue 1: 63 < 96 Clue 2: 3 and 7 are factors of 63 because 21 x 3 = 63 and 9 x 7 = 63. Clue 3: 63 ÷ 2 = 31 R 1. Clue 4: 63 ≠ 21. Clue 5: 20 ≤ 63 **5.** 1963

Solve It: Inventions
1. Look: There are 5 clues about the value of K. Clues 2 and 5 give information about the greatest and least values of K. The value of K completes the year that the ATM was invented. **2.** Plan and Do: From Clues 2 and 5, K is 50, 51, 52, ..., or 74. Clue 4 eliminates all numbers except for 51, 54, 57, 60, 63, 66, 69, and 72. Clue 3 eliminates 51, 54, 60, 63, and 72, leaving 57, 66, and 69. Clue 1 eliminates 57 and 66. K is 69. **3.** Answer and Check: K is 69. The ATM was invented in 1969. Check: Replace K with 69. Clue 1: 9 – 6 = 3 and 3 > 2. Clue 2: 50 ≤ 69. Clue 3: 6 + 9 = 15 and 15 > 11. Clue 4: 69 is a multiple of 3 because 23 x 3 = 69. Clue 5: 69 < 75

Perplexing Patterns (pages 22–30)
Solve the Problem
1. Ima saw that the numbers in Row 2 are consecutive multiples of 4. **2.** 20 x 4, or 80 **3.** (20 x 4) – 1, or 79 **4.** (30 x 4) – 1, or 119 **5.** (50 x 4) – 1, or 199

Make the Case
Whose circuits are connected? Boodles

Problem 1
1. Ima saw that the numbers in Row 2 are consecutive multiples of 3. **2.** 15 x 3, or 45 **3.** 45 – 1 = 44 **4.** (25 x 3) – 1 = 74 **5.** (30 x 3) – 1 = 89

Problem 2
1. Ima saw that the numbers in Row 3 are consecutive multiples of 6. **2.** 10 x 6, or 60 **3.** 60 – 2 = 58 **4.** (15 x 6) – 2 = 88 **5.** (20 x 6) – 2 = 118

Problem 3
1. 210 **2.** 208 **3.** The number in Row 1 below the 30th number in Row 3 is two less than 30 x 7; (30 x 7) – 2 = 208. **4.** (40 x 7) – 2, or 278 **5.** Multiply the position number by 7 and subtract 2 from the product.

Problem 4
1. 180 **2.** 177 **3.** The number in Row 1 below the 20th number in Row 4 is three less than 20 x 9; (20 x 9) – 3 = 177. **4.** (25 x 9) – 3, or 222 **5.** Multiply the position number by 9 and subtract 3 from the product.

Problem 5
1. 240 **2.** 237 **3.** The number in Row 1 below the 24th number in Row 4 is three less than 24 x 10; (24 x 10) – 3 = 237. **4.** (30 x 10) – 3, or 297 **5.** Multiply the position number by 10 and subtract 3 from the product.

Problem 6
1. 240 **2.** 236 **3.** The number in Row 1 below the 30th number in Row 5 is four less than 30 x 8; (30 x 8) – 4 = 236. **4.** (50 x 8) – 4 = 396 **5.** Number in Row 1 = (*P* x 8) – 4

Problem 7
1. 110 **2.** 106 **3.** The number in Row 1 below the 10th number in Row 5 is four less than 10 x 11; (10 x 11) – 4 = 106. **4.** 30 x 11 – 4 = 326 **5.** Number in Row 1 = (11 x *P*) – 4

Solve It: Perplexing Patterns
1. Look: There is an array with four rows of counting numbers. The numbers in Row 4 are consecutive multiples of 12. The problem is to figure out what number in Row 1 is below the 21st number in Row 4. **2.** Plan and Do: The numbers in Row 4 are multiples of 12. The 21st number in Row 4 is 21 x 12, or 252. The numbers in Row 1 below multiples of 12 are each three less than the multiple. (21 x 12) – 3, or 249. **3.** Answer and Check: 249. To check the computation, think of 21 as 20 + 1. So, 21 x 12 is the same as (20 x 12) + (1 x 12) = 240 + 12, or 252. Three less than 252 is 249.

Ticket Please (pages 33–41)
Solve the Problem
1. $3.00 **2.** $5.00 **3.** $2.00 **4.** In Clue 1, the total cost of the 3 senior tickets is $13.50 – $4.50, or $9.00, and each one is $9.00 ÷ 3, or $3.00. In Clue 2, replace each senior ticket with its cost of $3.00. Then 5 x $3.00, or $15.00, is the total cost of the 3 adult tickets, and each one is $15.00 ÷ 3, or $5.00. In Clue 3, replace the adult ticket and the 3 senior tickets with their costs. Then the 2 child tickets are $9.00 – $5.00, or $4.00, and each one is $4.00 ÷ 2, or $2.00.

Make the Case
Whose circuits are connected?
Mighty Mouth

Problem 1
1. $5.00 **2.** $6.00 **3.** $8.00 **4.** In Clue 3, a child ticket costs $11.00 – $6.00, or $5.00. In Clue 2, replace each child ticket with its cost. Then the total cost of 5 senior tickets is 6 x $5.00, or $30.00, and each one is $30.00 ÷ 5, or $6.00. In Clue 1, replace the senior and child tickets with their costs. Then the 2 adult tickets cost (2 x $5.00) + $6.00, or $16.00, and each one is $16.00 ÷ 2, or $8.00.

Problem 2
1. $6.00 **2.** $4.00 **3.** $3.00 **4.** In Clue 2, the total cost of 2 adult tickets and the $5.00 book is $17.00. So, the total cost of the 2 adult tickets is $17.00 – $5.00, or $12.00, and each one is $12.00 ÷ 2, or $6.00. In Clue 3, replace each adult ticket with its cost. Then, the total cost of the 3 senior tickets is 2 x $6.00, or $12.00, and each one is $12.00 ÷ 3, or $4.00. In Clue 1, replace each senior ticket with its cost. Then the total cost of the 4 child tickets is 3 x $4.00, or $12.00, and each one is $12.00 ÷ 4, or $3.00.

Problem 3
1. $5.50 **2.** $4.00 **3.** $6.50 **4.** In Clue 1, the 2 senior tickets are $11.00, so each one is $11.00 ÷ 2, or $5.50. In Clue 2, replace each senior ticket with its cost. Then the total cost of the 3 child tickets and the $4.50 roll of film is 3 x $5.50, or $16.50, and the 3 child tickets are $16.50 – $4.50, or $12.00. Each one is $12.00 ÷ 3, or $4.00. In Clue 3, replace the senior and child tickets with their costs. Then, 2 adult tickets + $11.00 = $24.00, and the 2 adult tickets are $24.00 – $11.00, or $13.00. Each one is $13.00 ÷ 2, or $6.50.

Problem 4
1. $7.50 **2.** $10.00 **3.** $4.00 **4.** In Clue 3, the total cost of 4 senior tickets and a set of $10.00 ear plugs is $40.00, so the 4 senior tickets are $40.00 – $10.00, or $30.00. Each one is $30.00 ÷ 4, or $7.50. In Clue 2, replace each senior ticket with its cost. Then the total cost of 3 adult tickets is 4 x $7.50, or $30.00, and each one is $30.00 ÷ 3, or $10.00. In Clue 1 replace the senior and adult tickets with their costs. Then $10.00 + 2 child tickets = (2 x $7.50) + $3.00, and 2 child tickets cost $18.00 – $10.00, or $8.00. Each one is $8.00 ÷ 2, or $4.00.

Problem 5
1. $9.00 **2.** $2.50 **3.** $6.50 **4.** In Clue 2, the total cost of 3 adult tickets is $30.00 – (2 x $1.50), or $27.00, and each one is $27.00 ÷ 3, or $9.00. In Clue 3, replace the adult ticket with its cost. Then the 2 child tickets are $14.00 – $9.00, or $5.00, and each one is $5.00 ÷ 2, or $2.50. In Clue 1, replace the adult and child tickets with their costs. Then (2 x $9.00) = 2 senior tickets + (2 x $2.50). So, $18.00 = 2 senior tickets + $5.00. So, each pair of senior tickets are $18.00 – $5.00, or $13.00, and each one is $13.00 ÷ 2, or $6.50.

Problem 6
1. $3.75 **2.** $9.50 **3.** $7.25 **4.** In Clue 1, the total cost of 2 child tickets is $20.00 – (2 x $6.25), or $7.50, and each ticket is $7.50 ÷ 2, or $3.75. In Clue 3, replace each child ticket with its cost. Then the 2 adult tickets are (4 x $3.75) + $4.00, or $19.00, and each adult ticket is $19.00 ÷ 2, or $9.50. In Clue 2, replace the child and adult tickets with their costs. Then $3.75 + (2 x $9.50) + the senior ticket = $30.00. So, the senior ticket is $30.00 – $22.75, or $7.25.

Problem 7
1. $6.25 **2.** $8.75 **3.** $5.00 **4.** In Clue 3, the 2 senior tickets are $28.00 – $8.00 – $7.50, or $12.50, and each one is $12.50 ÷ 2, or $6.25. In Clue 2, replace each senior ticket with its cost. Then 2 adult tickets + (2 x $6.25) = $30. So, the 2 adult tickets are $30.00 – $12.50, or $17.50. Each one is $17.50 ÷ 2, or $8.75. In Clue 1, the 3 child tickets = $8.75 + $6.25, or $15.00. So, each one is $15.00 ÷ 3, or $5.00.

Solve It: Ticket Please
1. Look: Three clues are given about the costs of child, adult, and senior tickets to the cactus garden. Clue 2 gives the total cost for 4 adult tickets and 4 bottles of water. Clue 3 gives the total cost of 2 adult tickets and 2 senior tickets. Clue 1 shows that the total cost of 3 senior and 3 child tickets is equal to the total cost of 2 adult tickets and a $9.00 cactus plant. **2.** Plan and Do. Begin with Clue 2 that shows the total cost of only one type of ticket. The cost of 4 adult tickets is equal to $38.00 – (4 x $1.25), or $33.00. So each one is $33.00 ÷ 4, or $8.25. In Clue 3, replace each adult ticket with its cost. Then the total cost of 2 senior tickets is $27.00 – (2 x $8.25), or $10.50. So each one is $10.50 ÷ 2, or $5.25. In Clue 1, replace the senior and the adult tickets with their costs: (3 x $5.25) + 3 child tickets = (2 x $8.25) + $9.00, or $15.75 + 3 child tickets = $25.50. Then 3 child tickets are $25.50 – $15.75, or $9.75. So, each one is $9.75 ÷ 3, or $3.25. **3.** Answer and Check: An adult ticket is $8.25. A senior ticket is $5.25. A child ticket is $3.25. To check, replace each ticket in the clues with its cost. Clue 1: (3 x $5.25) + (3 x $3.25) = (2 x $8.25) + $9.00; $15.75 + $9.75 = $16.50 + $9.00; and $25.50 = $25.50. Clue 2: (4 x $8.25) + (4 x $1.25) = $38.00; $33.00 + $5.00 = $38.00; and $38.00 = $38.00. Clue 3: (2 x $8.25) + (2 x $5.25) = $27.00; $16.50 + $10.50 = $27.00; and $27.00 = $27.00.

Blocky Balance (pages 44–52)
Solve the Problem
1. Ima started with the first pan balance because she could figure out that 2 spheres will balance 1 cylinder. Then she could substitute 2 spheres for each cylinder on the second pan balance **2.** 4 **3.** In the first pan balance, 4 spheres balance 2 cylinders, so 2 spheres (4 ÷ 2)

balance 1 cylinder (2 ÷ 2). In the second pan balance, substitute 2 spheres for each cylinder. Then 12 spheres balance the 4 cubes. **4.** 6 pounds **5.** 2 pounds

Make the Case
Whose circuits are connected?
CeCe Circuits

Problem 1
1. Ima started with the second pan balance because she could figure out that 1 sphere balances 2 cylinders. Then in the first pan balance, she could substitute 2 cylinders for each sphere. **2.** 8 **3.** In the second pan balance, 3 spheres balance 6 cylinders, so 1 sphere (3 ÷ 3) balances 2 cylinders (6 ÷ 3). In the first pan balance, substitute 2 cylinders for each sphere. Then 8 cylinders (4 x 2) will balance the 3 cubes. **4.** 8 pounds **5.** 3 pounds

Problem 2
1. Ima started with the second pan balance because she could figure out that 1 cylinder balances 2 cubes. Then in the first pan balance, she could substitute 2 cubes for each cylinder. **2.** 6 **3.** In the second pan balance, 2 cylinders balance 4 cubes, so 1 cylinder (2 ÷ 2) balances 2 cubes (4 ÷ 2). In the first pan balance, substitute 2 cubes for each cylinder. Then 6 cubes (3 x 2) will balance the 2 spheres. **4.** 18 pounds **5.** 4 pounds

Problem 3
1. Ima started with the first pan balance because she could figure out that one cube balances 2 spheres. Then in the second pan balance, she could substitute 2 spheres for each cube. **2.** 10 **3.** 20 **4.** In the first pan balance, 2 cubes balance 4 spheres, so one cube (2 ÷ 2) balances 2 spheres (4 ÷ 2). In the second pan balance, substitute 2 spheres for each cube. Then 10 spheres (5 x 2) will balance 3 cylinders. And 20 spheres (2 x 10) will balance 6 cylinders (2 x 3). **5.** 10 pounds

Problem 4
1. 3 **2.** 15 **3.** 30 **4.** In the first pan balance, 2 cylinders balance 6 cubes, so 1 cylinder (2 ÷ 2) balances 3 cubes (6 ÷ 2). In the second pan balance, substitute 3 cubes for each cylinder. Then 15 cubes (5 x 3) will balance 2 spheres. And 30 cubes (2 x 15) will balance 4 spheres (2 x 2). **5.** 2 pounds

Problem 5
1. 2 **2.** 8 **3.** 24 **4.** In the second pan balance, 3 spheres balance 6 cubes, so 1 sphere (3 ÷ 3) balances 2 cubes (6 ÷ 3). In the first pan balance, substitute 2 cubes for each sphere. Then 8 cubes will balance 3 cylinders. And 24 cubes (3 x 8) will balance 9 cylinders (3 x 3). **5.** 16 pounds

Problem 6
1. 2 **2.** 3 **3.** 9 **4.** In the first pan balance, 4 cubes balance 8 spheres, so 1 cube (4 ÷ 4) balances 2 spheres (8 ÷ 4). In the second pan balance, substitute one cube for every 2 spheres. Then 3 cubes will balance 4 cylinders. And 9 cubes (3 x 3) will balance 12 cylinders (3 x 4). **5.** 12 pounds

Problem 7
1. 2 **2.** 5 **3.** 15 **4.** In the second pan balance, 3 cylinders balance 6 cubes, so 1 cylinder (3 ÷ 3) balances 2 cubes (6 ÷ 3). In the first pan balance, substitute 1 cylinder for every 2 cubes. Then 2 cylinders will balance 5 spheres. And 6 cylinders (3 x 2) will balance 15 spheres (3 x 5). **5.** 20 pounds

Solve It: Blocky Balance
1. Look: There are two pan

balances. In the first pan balance, 5 cubes balance 6 spheres. In the second pan balance, 10 spheres balance 5 cylinders. The problem is to figure out how many cylinders will balance 10 cubes. **2.** Plan and Do: In the second pan balance, since 10 spheres balance 5 cylinders, then 2 spheres (10 ÷ 5) will balance 1 cylinder (5 ÷ 5). In the first pan balance, substitute 1 cylinder for every 2 spheres. Then 5 cylinders will balance 5 cubes, and 6 cylinders (2 x 3) will balance 10 cubes (2 x 5). **3.** Answer and Check: 6 cylinders will balance 10 cubes. To check, replace each cylinder with a weight, say for example, 10 pounds. Then determine the weights of the other blocks and the total weight in each pan. The total weight of each pan in the same pan balance must be the same. Second Pan Balance: If a cylinder is 10 pounds, then a sphere is 5 pounds; 5 x 10 = 10 x 5. First Pan Balance: Since a sphere is 5 pounds, then a cube is 12 pounds; 5 x 12 = 6 x 10.

In Good Shape (pages 55–63)
Solve the Problem
1. To figure out the perimeter of Clara's rectangle, you need to know the width of Moe's rectangle. To figure out the width of Moe's rectangle, you need to know the width of Avery's rectangle. P = l + l + w + w. For Avery's rectangle, 30 = 9 + 9 + w + w, and w + w = 12 in. So w = 12 ÷ 2, or 6 in. **2.** 3 in. **3.** 7 in. **4.** 6 in. **5.** Work backward. The perimeter of a rectangle = l + l + w + w. From Avery's fact, 30 = 9 + 9 + w + w, 30 = 18 + 2w, 12 = 2w, and w = 12 ÷ 2, or 6 in. From Moe's fact, the width of his rectangle is ½ x 6, or 3 in. From Clara's fact, her rectangle is 2 x 3, or 6 in. wide. Its length is 2 x 6 or 12 in., and its perimeter is (2 x 6) + (2 x 12), or 36 in.

Make the Case
Whose circuits are connected?
CeCe Circuits

Problem 1
1. Since P = 36 in., each side is 36 ÷ 4, or 9 in. So, l = w = 9 in. **2.** 5 in. **3.** l = 21 in.; w = 7 in. **4.** Work backward. Polly's fact: Each side of her square is 9 in. Earl's fact: His rectangle has a perimeter of ½ 36, or 18 in. Mac's fact: The length of his rectangle is 21 in. and the width is 7 in. The perimeter of Mac's rectangle is (2 x 7) + (2 x 21), or 56 in.

Problem 2
1. The length of Ella's rectangle is 6 in. and its area is 48 sq. in. So, 6 x w = 48, and w = 48 ÷ 6, or 8 in. With the length and width, the perimeter can be computed. **2.** 28 in. **3.** 38 in. **4.** Work backward. Ella's fact: w = 8 in. Joe's fact: w = 2 x 8, or 16 in. Ira's fact: w = ¼ x 16, or 4 in. Since 4 x l = 24 sq. in., l = 6 in. P = (2 x 4) + (2 x 6). So, P = 8 + 12, or 20 in.

Problem 3
1. The area of Justin's square is 64 sq. in., so each side is 8 in.; l = 8 in. and w = 8 in. **2.** 4 in. **3.** Work backward. Justin's fact: The l and w of the square are both 8 in. Isadora's fact: A = ½ x 64, or 32 sq. in.; l = 4 in. and w = 8 in. Minnie's fact: w = ½ x 8, or 4 in. Since P = 22 in., l + l + 4 + 4 = 22, and l = 7 in. A = 4 x 7, or 28 sq. in.

Problem 4
1. The width of Pete's rectangle is 4 in. Its length is 4 x 4, or 16 in. **2.** 8 in. **3.** 4 in. **4.** 2 sq. in; Work backward. Pete's fact: The width of his rectangle is 4 in. and its length is 16 in. Dee's fact: Her rectangle is ½ 16, or 8 in. long and 2 in. wide. (A = 8 x 2, or 16 sq. in.) Uriel's fact: The width of his rectangle is ½ x 8, or 4 in. and its length is 8 in. (A = 4 x 8, or 32 sq. in.) Ray's rectangle is ½ x 4, or

2 in. long and ½ x 2, or 1 in. wide. Its area is 1 x 2, or 2 sq. in.

Problem 5
1. 40 sq. in. (5 x 8 = 40 sq. in.) **2.** 28 in. = (2 x 12) + (2 x 2) in. **3.** 28 in. = (2 x 4) + (2 x 10) in. **4.** w = 2 in. and P = 16 in. **5.** Work backward. Tim's fact: l = 8 in. Shelley's fact: w = ¼ x 8, or 2 in. Sarah's fact: w = ⅓ x 12, or 4 in. Jack's fact: w = 4 – 2, or 2 in. l = 3 x 2, or 6 in. P = (2 x 6) + (2 x 2), or 16 in.

Problem 6
1. 20 in. **2.** 12 sq. in. **3.** 26 in. **4.** 22 in. **5.** Work backward. Dorie's fact: l = 6 in. and w = 4 in. May's fact: l = ⅓ x 6, or 2 in. and w = 6 in. Lon's fact: w = ⅓ x 6, or 2 in. Tamara's fact: A = 22 + 6, or 28 sq. in. w = (3 x 2) + 1, or 7 in.; l = 4 in.; P = (2 x 7) + (2 x 4), or 22 in.

Problem 7
1. 30 in. **2.** 26 sq. in. **3.** 48 sq. in. **4.** 14 in. **5.** Alex's fact: w = 5 in. and l = 10 in. P = (2 x 10) + (2 x 5) = 30 in. Parker's fact: l = ⅕ x 10, or 2 in., and P = 30 in. Tom's fact: l = 2 x 2, or 4 in. Since P = 32 in., w = 4 x 12, or 48 sq. in. Rhoda and Rita's fact: A = ¼ x 48, or 12 sq. in. l = 4 in. and w = 3 in., so P = (2 x 4) + (2 x 3), or 14 in.

Solve It: In Good Shape
1. Look: To figure out the perimeter of Carmen's rectangle, we have to know the length of Bill's rectangle. To get that measurement, we need to figure out the area of Jo's rectangle. To get that measurement, we need to figure out the length of Sonny's rectangle, so start with Sonny's fact. **2.** Plan and Do: Work backward. Sonny's rectangle has a length of 8 in. and a width of 7 in. Jo's rectangle is 8 in. long and 2 in. wide and has an area of 8 x 2, or 16 sq. in. Bill's rectangle has an area of ½ 16, or 8 sq. in.; its length is 4 in. and its width is 2 in. Carmen's rectangle has a length of 3 x 4, or 12 in. Its width is 6 in. because 12 x 6 = 72 sq. in. P = (2 x 6) + (2 x 12), or 36 in. **3.** Answer and Check: Carmen's rectangle has a perimeter of 36 in. To check, use the dimensions of each rectangle and check them with the facts. They must make sense.

Numbagliphics (pages 66–74)
Solve the Problem
1. By replacing the A, B, and A with 21, Ima can figure out the value of the other A. Since A + B + A is 21, the value of the other A is 27 – 21, or 6. **2.** 9 **3.** 7 **4.** From the third column, A + B + A is 21. In the first column, replace the A, B, and A with 21. Then the extra A is 27 – 21, or 6. In the first column, replace each A with 6. Then the B is 27 – 6 – 6, or 9. In the second column, replace the B and A with 15. Then the two Cs are 29 – 15, or 14, and C is 14 ÷ 2, or 7. **5.** 50

Make the Case
Whose circuits are connected?
Boodles

Problem 1
1. By replacing G and F with 9, she can figure out the value of the other F. Since G + F is 9, the value of the other two Fs is 13 – 9, or 4, and each F is 4 ÷ 2, or 2. **2.** 7 **3.** In the second column, G + F = 9. In the third column, replace G + F with 9. Then the other two Gs are 23 – 9, or 14, and each G is 14 ÷ 2, or 7. **4.** 23 **5.** 7

Problem 2
1. By replacing I, H, and I with 10, she can figure out the value of the other I. Since I + H + I is 10, the value of the other I in the third column is 3. **2.** 4 **3.** 8 **4.** From the second column, I + H + I = 10. Replace I, H, and I in the third column with 10. Then the extra I is 13

– 10, or 3. In the third column the three Is are 3 x 3, or 9. Then H is 13 – 9, or 4. In the first column, replace the I with 3 and each H with 4. Then J is 19 – 4 – 3 – 4, or 8. **5.** 6

Problem 3
1. By replacing M, L, and L with 23 in the third column, she can figure out the value of the other M. Since M, L, and L is 23, the other M is 26 – 23, or 3. **2.** 10 **3.** 6 **4.** From the first column, M + L + L is 23. Replace M, L, and L in the third column with 23. Then the extra M is 26 – 23, or 3. In the first column, replace M with 3. Then L + L is 30 – 7 – 3, or 20, and each L is 10. In the second column, replace each M with 3 and the L with 10. Then K is 22 – 3 – 3 – 10, or 6. **5.** 5

Problem 4
1. 7 **2.** 10 **3.** 9 **4.** In the third column, 4 + N + P + P = 32, so N + P + P is 32 – 4, or 28. Replace the N, P, and P with 28 in the second column. Then O is 35 – 28, or 7. Replace each O in the first column with 7. Then N + N = 34 – 7 – 7, or 20, and each N is 10. In the third column, replace the N with 10. Then P + P = 32 – 4 – 10, or 18, and each P is 9. **5.** 7

Problem 5
1. 15 **2.** 8 **3.** 11 **4.** In the first column, R + 9 + Q + Q = 40, so R + Q + Q is 31. In the second column, replace R, Q, and Q with 31. Then the extra R is 46 – 31, or 15. In the second column, replace each R with 15. Then Q + Q = 46 – 15 – 15, or 16 and each Q is 8. In the third column, replace the Q with 8. Then S + S + S is 41 – 8, or 33, and each S is 11. **5.** 15

Problem 6
1. 4 **2.** 12 **3.** 13 **4.** In the second column, T + U + 5 + T = 33, so T + U + T is 28. In the third column, replace T, U, and T with 28. Then the extra U is 32 – 28, or 4. In the third column, replace each U with 4. Then T + T is 32 – 4 – 4, or 24, and each T is 12. In the first column, replace each T with 12. Then V + V is 50 – 12 – 12, or 26, and each V is 13. **5.** 15

Problem 7
1. 18 **2.** 5 **3.** 9 **4.** In the third column, 17 + Y + W = 36, so Y + W + W is 19. In the first column, replace the Y, W, and W with 19. Then the X is 37 – 19, or 18. In the second column, replace each X with 18. Then W + W is 46 – 18 – 18, or 10, and each W is 5. In the third column, replace each W with 5. Then the Y is 36 – 17 – 5 – 5, or 9. **5.** 20

Solve It: Numbagliphics
1. Look: The cube has three columns of symbols. The numbers on the tops of the columns are the sums of the numbers or the values of the symbols in the columns. The first column sum is 62, the second column sum is 56, and the third column sum is 58. There are three different symbols. The first column contains the number 21. **2.** Plan and Do: First, subtract the 21 from the sum in the first column. Then Z + % + $ = 62 – 21, or 41. Second, replace the Z, %, and $ with 41 in the second column. The extra Z is 56 – 41, or 15. Third, in the third column, replace each Z with 15. Then % + % is 58 – 15 – 15, or 28, and each % is 14. Fourth, in the first column, replace the Z with 15 and the % with 14. Then the $ is 62 – 15 – 14 – 21, or 12. **3.** Answer and Check: The Z is 15, the $ is 12, and the % is 14. To check, replace each symbol with its value and add. Check the sums with the numbers on the tops of the columns. 15 + 14 + 21 + 12 = 62; 14 + 15 + 15 + 12 = 56; and 14 + 15 + 14 + 15 = 58.